P9-CQS-346

LOW MAINTENANCE
PERENNIALS

ROBERT S. HEBB

Drawings by ROBERT OPDYKE

Photographs by author unless otherwise indicated

Arnold Arboretum
of
Harvard University

Reprinted from Vol. 34, No. 5 and Vol. 35, No. 1 of *Arnoldia*, a publication of the Arnold Arboretum of Harvard University, Jamaica Plain, Massachusetts 02130

Copyright © 1974 and 1975 by the President and Fellows of Harvard College

1·617· 524·1718 ·

Some Necessary Definitions

Terms May Be Misleading

By definition, a perennial is a plant which lives on from year to year, not completing its life cycle in a single season as annuals do; or in two years, as with biennials. Properly applied, the term "perennial" includes trees, shrubs, and herbs. Trees and shrubs are woody; herbs die to the ground each winter.

The term "herb" is loosely used by many gardeners in referring to a special group of plants grown for culinary or medicinal purposes. While some of these plants are perennials, others are annuals or biennials; some are woody perennials and could not be classed as "herbs" according to the botanical definition of the word.

Perennial herbs are classified in many other ways, and terms become even more confusing when we consider the special uses of plants in the garden. Some perennial herbs are grown in a place called the "wild flower garden." These may be plants that are native locally, or come from much wider geographic areas and have cultural requirements similar to the plants of the local region. Other perennial herbs either require, or will tolerate, a great deal of moisture and, when grown together in a wet place, may constitute a bog garden. Others may be low in stature or will endure hot, dry conditions. When, in various ways, they are combined with rocks or boulders and certain shrubs, they form a rock garden.

Plants in all the categories above have representatives that, when planted closely under just the right conditions, grow together densely and tend to discourage competition from other plants. Under these circumstances they qualify as ground covers.

Obviously, perennial herbs cannot be considered always in separate categories. One group we have not discussed yet is the subject of this Handbook: the plants traditionally known as "herbaceous perennials", or just "perennials", and customarily grown in a place called the "perennial garden" or the "herbaceous border." This group draws representatives from all the above groups of perennial herbs, and its members are most often cultivated for their bright flowers; but plants with interesting foliage effects also are included.

The very word "perennial" conjurs up the idea of permanence, and to those who would make a perennial garden the great trap is that permanence is equated all too often with ease of culture or freedom from a great deal of maintenance. In his *Standard Cyclopedia of Horticulture*, Liberty Hyde Bailey succinctly sums up the problem as follows:

> A popular fallacy about perennials lies in the common statement that "they die down every year and come up again in the spring." Many of them never come up again after two or three years of flowering; that is *perennials are not necessarily perpetual.* (our emphasis) Peonies may be as long-lived as shrubbery, and a clump of fraxinella * has been known to outlive father, son, and grandson in the same spot. But these are exceptions. The general practice with perennials is to divide them every second or third year. Nearly all hardy herbaceous plants should be lifted now and then, because the crowns that give the flowers in most desirable kinds flower only two or three seasons and then die; but the plant may be continually spreading and making new growths, which furnish the flowers, and, unless lifted and divided, the stocks become scattering and unattractive.

Standards for Low Maintenance Perennials

Another feature of these plants that the word "perennial" does not convey is that many have exacting requirements which must be catered to if any degree of perfection whatever is to be attained. The cultivation of several of such types together in the same garden will add up to a lot of work; certainly more work than the novice gardener, or even the experienced one with little spare time, would wish to devote.

Some of the "faults" many perennials have which will necessitate considerable maintenance can be itemized as follows:

— Short-lived.
— Require annual or biennial division of the crowns.
— Become invasive.
— Subject to attack by insects or diseases.

* *Dictamnus albus*, the Gas Plant

— Need staking and tying to prevent flopping.
— Foliage does not remain attractive during the entire grow-
    ing season.
— Tolerate only a very narrow range of growing conditions
    with regard to soil, moisture, or light.
— Not fully hardy.

Possession of any of the above "faults", with the exception of
the last, is probably not sufficient reason in every case to ban
particular plants from the garden, even when the standard for
minimal maintenance is a priority. If this were so, the list
of perennials that could be grown would be a scanty one in-
deed! It is when certain plants combine two or more of these
"faults" that they may be regarded as requiring considerable
maintenance.

To look on the brighter side, there are many perennials that
possess the endearing qualities of ease of culture, a relatively
long life, and freedom from insects and diseases. However, the
gardener who lacks years of experience faces the very considerable problem of selecting these from amongst the many hundreds of varieties available from nurseries. Catalogs are no-
torious for their glowing descriptions of flower color, or any
other good attribute a plant may possess; however, information
about the amount of work necessary to produce a dazzling display or the life expectancy of a plant is mighty scanty. This is
not meant to discredit the nurserymen. In general, American
nurseries are doing a fine job of offering the better species or
selections to a very heterogeneous group of gardeners.

Textbooks too, are not always the most convenient sources of
information about low maintenance perennials. They often tend
to be encyclopedic in nature — some even include varieties
that are completely unavailable from nurseries. For the average
reader it thus becomes tedious to select those plants that are
easiest to grow from the numerous varieties described, and the
lengthy cultural formulae provided.

In this discussion we wish to draw attention to the perennials
that will require the least amount of maintenance. We know
of no desirable plant, however, that can be expected to thrive
in the garden without some form of attention. This handbook,

therefore, should not be considered a "lazy man's guide" to perennials. The standards we have selected that qualify a plant as "easy" in the ensuing text are as follows:

— Will not require division for about four years under normal circumstances; some can go much longer.
— Perfectly hardy in the Boston area, though some form of winter protection is advisable for most perennials. (In this category we also place resistance to summer heat as a type of hardiness.)
— Immune to, or tolerant enough of, insect and disease problems so that spraying usually will not be necessary.
— Stems sufficiently sturdy so that staking may be avoided under most circumstances.
— Tolerant of a fairly wide variety of soil types and conditions.
— Foliage remains in acceptable condition through the growing season. If not, it dies down quickly and may be masked by surrounding plants.

In applying these standards, we banish some of the showiest of all perennials. Gone are the hybrid Delphiniums, most of the hardy Chrysanthemums, and Phloxes, Lupines, or Carnations, and many others traditional to the perennial garden. But how many traditional perennial gardens do we see nowadays? In our hurried times, perennials have come into some measure of disfavor because a few of the more famous ones are the most difficult to grow. People have tried them, have had good results only temporarily, and have given up altogether.

Recommended Perennials for
Low Maintenance

The perennials we recommend for ease of culture are described in this chapter. Representatives of most all the major groups discussed here have been tried at one time or another at the Case Estates of the Arnold Arboretum in the area known as the Low Maintenance Garden. This garden is situated in a frost pocket where winter temperatures may drop to $-20°$ F, or lower. Soil conditions in some parts of the garden are very moist, especially during the winter months, and some perennials are either killed or heaved out of the ground during alternate periods of freezing and thawing. Some sections of the garden receive full sun all day, while others remain either in partial or deep shade.

Thus we have been able to observe and record the performance of many perennials under adverse, and frequently poor, growing conditions. We make the basic assumption that a plant which has performed well for several years in the Low Maintenance Garden can be grown in most gardens in the Boston area, and often considerably further north.

In order that gardeners may make intelligent choices when selecting their plant materials, we discuss in alphabetical order most all the major genera of perennials offered by the nursery trade. Those that qualify as "easy" plants, and are especially recommended as low maintenance subjects, occupy the main body of the text. Those which are of secondary value (or of no value at all where low maintenance is concerned) are included, but set apart in smaller type. This secondary listing is in no way meant to condemn the groups of plants involved. As already stated, some of the most beautiful perennials belong in these groups. If a gardener has selected mainly the recommended plants, he then may have the time to cater to the needs of a few of the more demanding types if he so desires.

We have attempted to provide as many sources as possible for each plant discussed. Most of the nurseries included publish a retail catalog on a national basis and will ship plants. A few nurseries are represented which do not ship, but their lists are

[5]

so extensive that they warrant inclusion. Several desirable cultivars seem to be available only from wholesale nurseries, which will not deal directly with the general public. If this is the case with a plant you wish to obtain, we recommend that you persuade a local nurseryman to get it for you from the wholesaler; do not attempt to deal with wholesale nurseries directly. Wholesale sources are included here mainly for the benefit of the professional horticulturist or landscape architect entitled to use them or, hopefully, the operators of local retail outlets who may wish to extend their offerings to include some of the more desirable varieties discussed.

Retail nurseries are identified by a series of numbers after the description of each plant; wholesale nurseries, by a series of letters. These correspond to a list of the nurseries beginning on page 7. Before deciding to order a particular plant from any of these sources, it would be prudent first to see if it is available from a local garden center or nursery. It is always better to obtain a plant locally when possible; the plant's size and condition are then known to the buyer. Also, local nurseries frequently sell perennials already established in containers; therefore the possible shock of transplanting or delays in the mail can be avoided.

According to the listings which follow, it may appear that some worthy perennials have limited availability; that is, they are available only from one or two mail order nurseries. These listings do not present the true picture in every case, however. In all major population centers there are garden outlets or nurseries which operate on a local basis and do not distribute lists or catalogs. Thus some plants enjoy a popularity which our listings do not reflect.

Exclusion of a nursery is not intentional on our part. The listings were compiled from the hundred or more catalogs of American dealers in perennials currently represented in the Arnold Arboretum's catalog collection. It is quite possible that other sources exist of which we are not aware. We did not deem it expedient to list general nurseries which offer only four or five of the recommended varieties. Further, many specialists in rock garden plants and wild flowers list a few plants suitable for the perennial border; some of these dealers could not be included. There are far more nurseries specializing in *Iris, Hemerocallis,* or *Paeonia* than we could list. For more information about these, consult the advertisement sections of *The Hemerocallis Journal,* (the publication of the American Hemerocallis

Society), the *Bulletin of the American Iris Society*, and *The American Peony Society Bulletin*.

Inclusion here of a particular nursery does not constitute an endorsement by the Arnold Arboretum, nor does it guarantee that plants obtained will be true to name, nor that sources will not change from year to year.

RETAIL NURSERY SOURCES FOR HERBACEOUS PERENNIALS

1. J. Herbert Alexander, Dahliatown Nurseries, Middleboro, Mass. 02346.
Specializes in Lilacs, Blueberries, shrubs, ground covers and perennials. Ships.
2. Armstrong Nurseries, Inc., Box 473, Ontario, Calif. 91761.
Principally a grower of Roses, but catalog lists an interesting selection of Hardy Hibiscus. Ships.
3. Arrowhead Gardens, Inc., 115 Boston Post Rd., Wayland, Mass. 01778.
Extensive list of perennials, rock garden plants and others. Does not ship.
4. Avalon Mountain Gardens, Dana, N.C. 28724.
Extensive listings of perennials, wild flowers, and some woody plants. Ships.
5. Beersheba's Wild Flower Gardens, P.O. Box 551, Beersheba Springs, Pa. 37305.
Mostly wild flowers, but list includes a few perennials suited to the border. Ships.
6. Myron D. Bigger, 201 North Rice Rd., Topeka, Kan. 66616.
Specializes in Peonies, many of which are Mr. Bigger's own named varieties. Also Hemerocallis. Ships.
7. Blackthorne Gardens, 48 Quincy St., Holbrook, Mass. 02343.
Specializes mostly in bulbs, but also lists some perennials, particularly *Hosta*. Ships.
8. Brand Peony Farm, Box 36, Fourbault, Minn. 55021.
Specializes in Peonies, Iris, and Lilacs. Ships.
9. Bristol Nurseries, Inc., Bristol, Conn. 06101.
Specializes in hardy Chrysanthemums. Extensive list. Ships.
10. Brown's Sunnyhill Gardens, Route 3, Box 102, Milton-Freewater, Ore. 97862.
Specializes in Bearded Iris. Extensive list. Ships.
11. Burge's Iris Garden, 1414 Amhurst, Denton, Tex. 76201.
Specializes in Iris. Extensive list. Ships.
12. W. Atlee Burpee Co., Box 6929, Philadelphia, Pa. 19132.
The fall catalog, separate from the main seed catalog, lists bulbs and plants, including some perennials. Ships.
13. Carroll Gardens, Westminster, Md. 21157.
Extensive retail list of perennials of all kinds. Also herbs, ground covers, trees and shrubs. Separate wholesale list for perennials. Ships.

14. Conley's Garden Center, Inc., Boothbay Harbor, Me. 04538.
    General line of nursery stock, including perennials. These
    are mostly available at the garden center, only a few being
    included in the list of materials which can be shipped. The
    catalog has been very thoughtfully produced, and is a horti-
    cultural handbook in itself.

15. The Conard-Pyle Co., Star Roses, West Grove, Pa. 19390.
    Specialists in Roses. Catalog also offers a selection of peren-
    nials. Ships.

16. Cooley's Gardens, Silverton, Ore. 97381.
    Specializes in Bearded Iris. Extensive, profusely illustrated
    color catalog — $.50. Ships.

17. P. DeJager & Sons, Inc., South Hamilton, Mass. 01982.
    Catalog primarily lists bulbous plants, but sometimes in-
    cludes a few perennials. Ships.

18. Dooley Gardens, R.R. 1, Hutchinson, Minn. 55350.
    Specializes in Chrysanthemums. Ships.

19. Eden Road Iris Garden, P.O. Box 117, Wenatchee, Wash. 98801.
    Specializes in Bearded Iris. Extensive profusely illustrated
    color catalog — $.50. Ships.

20. Emlong's Nurseries, Inc., Stevensville, Mich. 49127.
    Catalog of general nursery items including a few perennials.
    Ships.

21. Englerth Gardens, Route 2, Hopkins, Mich. 49328.
    Specializes in *Hosta, Hemerocallis,* Siberian and Japanese
    Iris. Ships.

22. Far North Gardens, 14621 Auburndale Ave., Livonia, Mich.
    48154.
    Specializes in hardy Primroses, both plants and seed. Very
    extensive list. Ships.

23. Fowler's Nursery, 4210 Fayetville Rd., P.O. Box 10324, Raleigh,
    N.C. 27605.
    Perennials, bulbs, bedding plants, trees and shrubs. Ships in
    the southern states only.

24. Garden Place, 6780 Heisley Rd., Mentor, O. 44060.
    Extensive list of perennials of all kinds. This is the retail
    outlet for Springbrook Gardens, Inc. Ships.

25. Gurney Seed & Nursery Co., Yankton, S.D. 57078.
    Catalog of general nursery items, includes some perennials.
    Ships.

26. Ruth Hardy's Wildflower Nursery, Falls Village, Conn. 06031.
    Specializes in wild flowers and ferns. Some suited to the
    perennial border. Ships.

27. Hi-Mountain Farm, Seligman, Mo. 65745.
    Extensive list of wild flowers and ferns. Many suited to the
    perennial border. Ships.

28. Inter-State Nurseries, Hamburg, Ia. 51644.
    Catalog of general nursery items. Lists some perennials.
    Ships.

29. The Jamieson Valley Gardens, Jamieson Rd., R. 3, Spokane,
    Wash. 99203.
    Hardy perennials, alpines, wild flowers and Western native
    plants. Catalog $1.00, free with orders over $10.00. Ships.

30. Kelly Brothers Nurseries, Inc., Dansville, N.Y. 14437.
    Catalog of general nursery items. Includes some perennials.
    Ships.
31. Charles Klehm & Son, 2 East Algonquin Rd., Arlington Heights,
    Ill. 60005.
    Specializes in Peonies, especially the Estate Peonies developed
    at Klehm's. Extensive list. Ships.
32. Lamb Nurseries, E 101 Sharp Ave., Spokane, Wash. 99202.
    Extensive list of perennials of all kinds. Also rock garden
    plants, and some shrubs which combine well with perennials.
    Ships.
33. H. V. Lawrence, Inc., The Cape Cod Nurseries and Gardening
    Center, P.O. Drawer B, Falmouth, Mass. 02541.
    General nursery stock including perennials. Does not ship,
    but a good source for perennials on Cape Cod. (Apparently
    a catalog is no longer being published.)
34. The Lehman Gardens, Faribault, Minn. 55021.
    Extensive listing of hardy garden Chrysanthemums. Ships.
35. Lexington Gardens, 7007 Manchester Ave., Kansas City, Mo.
    64133.
    Specializes in *Hemerocallis*. Extensive list. Ships.
36. Mathews Iris Gardens, 201 Sunny Dr., College Place, Wash.
    99324.
    Specializes in Bearded Iris. Extensive list. Ships.
37. Earl May Seed & Nursery Co., Shenandoah, Ia. 51603.
    Catalog of general nursery items and seeds. Lists some pe-
    rennials. Ships.
38. Melrose Gardens, 309 Best Rd., South, Stockton, Calif. 95206.
    Specializes in Iris of all types. Extensive lists. Catalog $.35.
    Ships.
39. Mincemoyer Nursery, County Line Rd. (Route 526), Jackson,
    N.J. 08527.
    Perennials, wild flowers, herbs. Ships.
40. Mission Gardens, Highway 43 (Waukegan Rd.), Techny, Ill.
    60082.
    Specializes in Peonies (both herbaceous and tree types), and
    Hemerocallis. Extensive lists. Ships.
41. Mission Bell Gardens, 2778 West 5600 South, Roy, Ut. 84067.
    Specializes in Bearded Iris. Extensive list. Ships.
42. Moldovan's Gardens, 38830 Detroit Rd., Avon, O. 44011.
    Specializes in *Iris*, *Hemerocallis*, and Peonies. Ships.
43. Orchid Gardens, Route 3, Box 224, Grand Rapids, Mich. 55744.
    Specializes in native plants, but lists some suited to the
    perennial border. Catalog $.25. Ships.
44. George W. Park Seed Co., Inc., Greenwood, S.C. 29647.
    A catalog, separate from the main seed catalog, lists supplies,
    bulbs and plants, including some perennials. Ships.
45. Pellett Gardens, Atlantic, Ia. 50022.
    Specializes in plants which attract bees, but catalog also
    contains some plants useful in the perennial border. Ships.
46. Putney Nursery, Inc., Putney, Vt. 05346.
    Good list of perennials. Also wild flowers, ferns, herbs, trees,
    shrubs, and vines. Ships.

47. David L. Reath, Box 251, Vulcan, Mich. 49892.
    Specialist in Peonies, both the herbaceous and tree types.
    Ships.
48. Richland Iris Productions Ltd., Richland Center, Wis. 53581.
    Extensive list of Iris, including Siberian and Japanese types.
    Ships.
49. The Rock Garden, Litchfield-Hallowell Rd., RFD 2, Litchfield,
    Me. 04350.
    Extensive list of plants for the perennial border and the rock
    garden. Catalog states that listing may vary considerably
    every year. Ships.
50. Savage Gardens, P.O. Box 163, McMinnville, Tenn. 37110.
    Supplier of wild flowers and ferns, some appropriate to the
    perennial garden. Ships.
51. Savory's Greenhouses, 5300 Whiting Avenue, Edina, Minn.
    55435.
    Specializes in *Hosta*. Extensive list. Ships.
52. Schreiner's Gardens, 3625 Quinaby Rd., N.E., Salem, Ore. 97303.
    Specializes in Bearded Iris. Also Siberian and Spuria types.
    Extensive list. Catalog profusely illustrated in color. $.50.
    Ships.
53. R. H. Shumway, Rockford, Ill. 61101.
    General catalog of seeds and plants. Some perennials. Ships.
54. C. G. Simon Nursery, Inc., P.O. Box 2873, Lafayette, La. 70501.
    Specializes in *Hemerocallis*. Extensive list. Ships.
55. Smith's Iris Gardens, 614 Bryden Ave., Box 483, Lewiston, Ida.
    83501.
    Specializes in Bearded Iris. Extensive list. Ships.
56. Southern Meadows Garden, 1424 South Perrine, Walnut Hill
    Rd., P.O. Box 230, Centralia, Ill. 62801.
    Extensive list of Bearded Iris and *Hemerocallis*. Ships.
57. Sperka's Woodland Acres Nursery R2, Crivitz, Wis. 54114.
    Perennials and wildflowers. Ships.
58. Spring Hill Nurseries, Tipp City, O. 45366.
    Catalog of general nursery items. Lists some perennials.
    Ships.
59. Stanek's Garden Center, East 2929 27th Ave., Spokane, Wash.
    99203.
    General line of nursery stock, includes a list of perennials.
    Ships.
60. Stern's Nurseries, Inc., Geneva, N.Y. 14456.
    General line of nursery stock. List includes some perennials.
    Catalog costs $.35. Ships.
61. Alex J. Summers, 14 I. V. Willets Rd. W., Roslyn, N.Y. 11576.
    Specializes in *Hosta*. Extensive list. Minimum order $20.00.
    Ships.
62. Sunnyslope Gardens, 8638 Huntington Dr., San Gabriel, Calif.
    91775.
    Specializes in Chrysanthemums of all types including hardy
    garden varieties. Ships.
63. Thomasville Nurseries, Inc., P.O. Box 7, Thomasville, Ga. 31792.
    Extensive listing of *Hemerocallis*. Ships.

64. Thon's Garden Mums, 4815 Oak St., Crystal Lake, Ill. 60014.
    Specializes in Chrysanthemums. Profusely illustrated color catalog. Ships.
65. Top O' The Ridge, 100 NE 81st St., Kansas City, Mo. 64118.
    Extensive listing of Peonies and Iris. Ships.
66. Martin Viette Nurseries, Northern Boulevard (25A), East Norwich, Long Island, N.Y. 11732.
    Probably the most extensive listing of perennials in this country. Exceptional lists of *Astilbe, Hosta,* ferns, grasses, herbs, *Hemerocallis, Iris, Phlox, Paeonia.* Does not ship.
67. The Wayside Gardens Co., Mentor, O. 44060.
    Catalog costs $2.00 but price is refundable on orders over $15.00. May be worth the price for color pictures alone. Extensive list of perennials of all kinds, also trees, shrubs, and vines. Ships.
68. Weston Nurseries, East Main St., Rte. 135, Hopkinton, Mass. 01748.
    Retail only, does not ship, but carries one of the most extensive selections of perennials in the Boston area. Also complete line of trees and shrubs.
69. White Flower Farm, Litchfield, Conn. 06759.
    Extensive list of perennials, shrubs, bulbs, etc. Catalog published spring and fall costs $3.00 but price is refundable on orders totaling $15.00. Catalog is a handbook in itself and gives good descriptions and cultural directions. Ships.
70. Gilbert H. Wild and Son, Inc., Sarcoxie, Mo. 64862.
    Specializes in Peonies, Bearded Iris, and *Hemerocallis.* Extensive lists. Catalog $1.00. Profusely illustrated in color. Ships.

WHOLESALE NURSERY SOURCES FOR HERBACEOUS PERENNIALS

(The following nurseries do not deal directly with the general public. Do not attempt to order plants from them. If a plant you wish to obtain is available only from one of these suppliers, have your local nurseryman order it for you.)

A — Bluebird Nursery & Greenhouse, 515 Linden St., Clarkson, Neb. 68629.
    General list of herbaceous perennials.
B — Bluemount Nurseries, Inc., 2103 Blue Mount Rd., Monkton, Md. 21111.
    Extensive list of perennials of all kinds, including ornamental grasses.
C — Carroll Gardens, Westminster, Md. 21157.
    Extensive list of perennials of all kinds. Separate retail catalog.
D — Cunningham Gardens, Waldron, Ind. 46182.
    Chrysanthemums, ground cover plants, Clematis.
E — Hauser's Superior View Farm, Bayfield, Wis. 54814.
    General list of perennials. Includes selection of named forms of Russell Hybrid Lupines.

[11]

F — Iverson Perennial Gardens, RR 1, Box 177, Palatine, Ill. 60067. General listing of perennials.

G — The Joseph F. Martin Company, Inc., 1500 W. Jackson St., P.O. Box 189, Painesville, O. 44077. General list of perennials and ground covers. Extensive list of Chrysanthemums.

H — Mount Arbor Nurseries, P.O. Box 129, Shenandoah, Ia. 51601. Primarily a grower of trees and shrubs, but offers a selection of herbaceous perennials, including Peonies.

I — Springbrook Gardens, Inc., 6776 Heisley Road, Mentor, O. 44060. Extensive list of perennials. Strictly wholesale, but Springbrook's retail mail order outlet is Garden Place.

J — Jack Vermeulen Nurseries, Route 1, Holland, Mich. 49423 or P.O. Box 296, Saugatuck, Mich. 49453. Perennials, ground covers, dwarf shrubs.

K — Walters Gardens Inc., P.O. Box 137, 96th Ave. at M-21, Zeeland, Mich. 49464. Extensive general list of perennials.

L — Weller Nurseries Company, P.O. Box 1111, Holland, Mich. 49423. Extensive list of perennials of all kinds. Particularly good list of Phlox. Also, ground covers and Clematis.

M — Dale Wild, Sarcoxie Nurseries, Inc., Peony Fields, P.O. Box. 306, Sarcoxie, Mo. 64862. Specializes in Peonies, Iris, and *Hemerocallis*. Extensive lists.

N — Yoder Brothers Inc., Barberton, O. 44203. Extensive catalog of Chrysanthemums and other plants for the commercial grower.

In Mulch Display Beds at the Case Estates, 20 different mulches suitable for use in herbaceous or shrub borders are on view in small rectangular beds. In addition, many perennials that have not been included in the Low Maintenance Garden may be seen here.

Low Maintenance Perennial Garden of the Arnold Arboretum at the Case Estates, Weston, Mass. Herbaceous perennials requiring a minimal amount of maintenance have been selected with care for this garden. They are displayed in free-form beds among shrubs that have attractive shapes, colors, or textures, giving the garden interest at every season of the year.

[13]

Achillea 'Coronation Gold'

Acanthus species — Distributed by a few nurseries, but not hardy in our area without considerable winter protection.

Achillea   **Yarrow, Milfoil, Sneezewort**
                         Daisy Family (Compositae)

Some members of this genus of the Daisy family are easy to grow, will live on in spite of considerable neglect, and are very hardy. All adapt well to poor garden soils. In fact, average to poor soil somewhat on the dry side is best for them; rich or moist soil conditions promote weak growth and inferior flowers. The ability to withstand drought in open, sunny locations and the finely textured, pungent, fernlike foliage which remains in good condition throughout the growing season are other points in their favor. Never plant any of this group in the shade.

Those called the Yarrows (mainly varieties of *A. filipendulina*, *A. millefolium*, and *A.* 'Taygeta') blossom for several weeks, and the flowers are excellent for cutting or drying; but beware of the claim in catalogs that they "bloom from June to the end of September." Recurrent flowering in this group is possible, but best results can only be achieved by faithful attention to the removal of the faded flowers to prevent seed formation.

A. filipendulina (syn. *A. eupatorium*) — Fernleaf Yarrow — Of value, but the named selections which follow have bigger, brighter flowers or are smaller in stature. The numerous small flowers of this group are yellow and are densely grouped in flattened saucer-shaped heads (corymbs) up to 4 to 6 inches across.

The species grows to a height of 3 to 4 feet. Plants may require staking unless given full sun and dry soil, especially if grown in a windy place. The grayish leaves are dissected and fernlike; blossoms appear in late June to mid-July, with recurrent flowers until September. Very drought-resistant with no insect or disease problems. Fernleaf Yarrows should be divided in spring after the fourth year to maintain vigorous growth. They are effective when planted either singly or in a group of three, 10 to 12 inches apart.
Sources: 3,4,46,68; L

A. filipendulina 'Gold Plate' — Largest and showiest of the group. Plants grow to 4 to 4½ feet with corymbs up to 6 inches across. Flowers bright yellow. Essential to have in a relatively dry place and away from strong winds to avoid staking. Especially fine for cut flowers. Culture same as for the species. Space 12 to 15 inches apart or as a single specimen.
Sources: 28,58,60

A. 'Coronation Gold' (*A. filipendulina* $\times$ 'Clypeolata') — Lower growing than *A. filipendulina* (2½ to 3 feet) and less likely to require staking. Mustard-yellow flowers and pleasing, finely divided, gray-green leaves. Long succession of flowers if seed formation is prevented. Culture and spacing the same as for the species.
Sources: 13,24,32,57,66,67,70C; I,J,K,L

A. 'Taygeta' — Lowest growing of the Yarrows recommended here, about 1½ feet. Handsome silvery leaves not as finely divided as those above. Flowers pale yellow, blooming over the same long period as the others. Culture the same; space in a group of three, 10 to 12 inches apart.
Sources: 24,66,69; B,L,T

A. 'Moonshine' — Selected form of A. 'Taygeta'. Flowers are a deeper, canary-yellow. Otherwise the same.
Sources: 3,24,32,49,66,67,68,69; C,I,K

A. millefolium — Milfoil or Common Yarrow — The species is a common weed of waste places and lawns where the soil is infertile; it is of questionable value in the perennial garden. The flowers are off-white. The selected forms which have flowers ranging from deep pink to rosy-red are, however, of interest, but must be placed second in value when compared to the usefulness of the varieties of *A. filipendulina* and *A.* 'Taygeta'. The flowers are borne in the same corymb-type inflorescence, but smaller to 2½ to 3 inches across, and the leaves are finely divided. Plants are about 1½ to 2 feet tall when in flower. Blossoming time is late June, July, and into September if the old flower heads are removed. These have a tendency to spread more than the other Yarrows; but if the soil is not rich, they cannot be classed as invasive. Full sun and a dry planting site are necessary. Somewhat ineffective as single specimens, they should be planted in groups of three about 12 inches apart, at the front of the garden. Staking will not be required, but division after the fourth year is recommended.

A. millefolium **'Crimson Beauty'** — Flowers rose-red. 18 inches tall.
Sources: 13,66; C

A. millefolium **'Fire King'** — Flowers deep rose-red. This is probably the most handsome of the *A. millefolium* cultivars. 18 inches tall.
Sources: 32,67,68,69

A. millefolium **'Red Beauty'** — Flowers red. Plants 18 inches tall.
Sources: 24,39,66; B,I

Achillea ptarmica — Sneezewort — All varieties not recommended for low maintenance. Require division every other year; in some situations, annually to maintain the clumps in good condition. Become invasive if not restrained by division. Flowers excellent for cutting.

Cultivars available include:

A. ptarmica **'Angel's Breath'** — Double white flowers.
Sources: 24,66,67,68; I,J,K,L

A. ptarmica **'Perry's Giant'** — Double white flowers.
Sources: 13; C

A. ptarmica **'The Pearl'** — Double white flowers.
Sources: 3,24,43,46,69; I,L

The following are sometimes listed by suppliers of perennials, but are better suited to the rock garden.

A. ageratifolia — Greek Yarrow — Flowers white. Plants 2 to 4 inches tall.
Sources: 66,69

A. ageratifolia var. *aizoon* (listed in catalogs as *Anthemis aizoon*) — Superior to the species. Flowers white. Plants 6 inches tall.
Sources: 3,24; I

A. tomentosa — Woolly Yarrow — Bright canary-yellow flowers; woolly gray-green leaves. Plants 10 inches tall. Spreads very rapidly.
Sources: 3,13,24,39,66; C,I

A. tomentosa **'Moonlight'** — Less invasive than the species. Flowers lighter yellow in color.
Sources: 49,66

A. × **'King Edward'** (*A. clavenae* × *A. tomentosa*) — Flowers, primrose-yellow; woolly, gray-green leaves. Plants 8 inches tall.
Sources: 24; I

Aconitum napellus — *Aconite Monkshood*

Aconitum   **Aconite, Monkshood, Wolf's Bane**
                              Buttercup Family (Ranunculaceae)

Plants which prefer to be left alone and yet do not outgrow their welcome must be considered valuable. When they also display attractive, glossy foliage throughout the season and provide conspicuous blue or purple flowers which are excellent for cutting, they deserve to be widely grown. Monkshoods qualify on all counts.

Attention is focused from time to time on the poisonous nature of these plants. Although it is true that no portion should be eaten, it is unlikely that humans would find occasion to taste either the leaves or roots. The tuberous roots are particularly virulent and could be confused with Jerusalem Artichokes or other root vegetables, however. For this reason, Monkshoods never should be grown near the vegetable garden; it also would be prudent not to plant them in areas frequented by small children.

Monkshoods are very hardy. They blossom in August and September, a time when most other plants with blue flowers have gone by, and the vertical effect, similar to that of Delphiniums, is particularly welcome. They require a fairly rich soil to which liberal amounts of compost have been added. If plants are grown in full sun, the soil must be moist, (not wet); drying out will check the growth and cause stunting. Aconites often do best in partial shade, or where they are exposed to full sun for only part of the day; however, they soon will decline in vigor if grown near trees providing root competition. Whatever the spot chosen, watering in really dry periods of the summer will be beneficial.

Clumps are easily divided either in early spring or autumn, but the plants are slow to increase and can be left for many years before division for rejuvenation, or to relieve crowding, will be necessary. About the only fault that can be found is that some of the taller varieties will require staking to prevent toppling from winds or rain. If the proper conditions can be provided, Monkshoods possess so many other good traits that this can be tolerated in a low maintenance situation.

Monkshoods are best seen as individual specimens planted about 2 feet from their nearest neighbors. According to variety, they are suited to the middle or rear of the border.

A. carmichaelii (syn. *A. fischeri*, the old name by which this is listed in catalogs) — Azure Monkshood — Grows to 2½ feet in sun and up to 3½ feet in shade, and is one of the lower varieties. Flowers pale blue from mid-August to mid-September, on stems strong enough to be self-supporting. Leaves large, smooth and lustrous, three-parted, with attractively divided segments.
Sources: 3,13,24,32,69; C,I

A. carmichaelii var. *Wilsonii* (syn. *A. fischeri* var. *Wilsonii*, the old name by which it is listed in catalogs) — Tallest of the group, towering to 6 to 8 feet depending on location; must be staked, otherwise easily toppled by wind or rain. Best sited at rear of the border. Violet-blue flowers during most of the month of September.
Sources: 24; I

A. carmichaelii var. *Wilsonii* 'Barker's Variety' — Grows 4 to 5 feet, and requires staking. An excellent color form, bright violet-blue or amethyst-blue flowers from late August to mid-September.
Sources: 24,69; I

A. napellus — Aconite Monkshood — Flowers may be variable from blue to violet. Has probably the most attractive, finely divided foliage of the group. Plants 3½ to 4 feet in height and may require some staking. Blossoms earlier than most in August and early September. This is said to be the most poisonous species.
Sources: 4,32,57

A. napellus var. *bicolor* — Considered to be better than the species because of the two-toned appearance of the flowers. Outer edges are bright blue and fade to white in the center. Leaves as finely divided as the species. Plants 3½ to 4 feet tall and may require staking.
Source: 32

A. napellus 'Spark's Variety' — Flowers deep violet-blue, on spikes 3 to 4 feet tall; they appear in August and last well into September. Secondary spikes extend the flowering season, but plants are likely to require staking.
Sources: 13,24,46,69; C,I

Adenophora   **Ladybells, Garland Bellflower**
                                    Bellflower Family (Campanulaceae)
A much underrated genus of the Campanula family. The
plants closely resemble the Campanulas or Bellflowers and to a
non-botanist are virtually indistinguishable. The following appears to be the only species presently offered by dealers in
perennials.

A. confusa (usually listed in catalogs as *A. farreri*) — Native to
China. Flowers deep blue on 30-inch spikes for a relatively long
time in July and August. Highly resents division or disturbance
of any sort, is long-lived and very hardy. Quite sturdy and will
not require staking. Does poorly in a dry soil and requires full
sun. Plant at the middle of the border, either singly or in groups
of three spaced 12 inches apart.
Sources: 24,69; I

Aethionema   **Stonecress**
                                Mustard Family (Cruciferae)
Frequently seen in catalogs which feature perennials, but best
suited to hot, dry areas of the rock garden.

Ajuga   **Bugle, Bugleweed**
                                    Mint Family (Labiatae)
Numerous varieties are offered, but are not recommended for
the herbaceous border as they spread rapidly and soon become
invasive — especially in the lawn where they are a great
nuisance.

Alchemilla vulgaris   **Lady's Mantle**
                                    Rose Family (Rosaceae)
This is a low growing plant suitable for the front of the border
and does equally well in sun or in partial shade. It does not like
dry soils, but otherwise is undemanding.
Although not outstanding, the yellowish-green or chartreuse
flowers in July on stems to 18 inches are interesting and unusual subjects, either fresh or dried in small bouquets. The
palmately-lobed, 3 to 4-inch-wide leaves are handsome throughout the growing season. They are somewhat hairy and rounded,
and the lobes are creased like the segments of a fan.

Clumps will last in good condition for many years, but by the third or fourth year will have enlarged sufficiently so that division for purposes of increase is possible, either in early spring or autumn. For best effect, plant in groups of at least three, spaced 10 inches apart. Larger groupings are effective as ground cover.
Sources: 24,69; I

A. alpina — Too diminutive for the perennial garden, but a choice subject in the rock garden. Grows to a height of 4 to 6 inches.
Sources: 49,57

Althaea rosea   Hollyhock
                                        Hibiscus Family (Malvaceae)
Although Hollyhocks are short-lived perennials (often best treated as biennials), they seed in so easily that plantings almost always perpetuate themselves. This tendency may make them unsuitable for well-groomed formal gardens, but most low maintenance situations should have a plant or two. Demonstrating their permanence is a spot in the Arnold Arboretum at the far side of Bussey Hill where the old Bussey Mansion once stood; the building was torn down over thirty years ago and today a mound of earth remains which is crowned in summer with Hollyhocks, and in spring with Snowdrops and Crocuses.

All that is required for successful cultivation of Hollyhocks is a well-drained soil of average fertility, and a site in full sun. Seedlings in unwanted places are easily controlled if discarded when young. The main enemy of Hollyhocks in our area is the Japanese Beetle. Also, Hollyhock rust is frequently a problem. This is a fungus disease which produces large orange spore cases on the leaves. A combination of these two problems produces very unsightly foliage and is the principal reason that Hollyhocks should be used sparingly.

Hollyhocks attain heights of 5 to 8 feet, and thus are suitable for the rear of the sunny garden. The flowers are borne all along the tall spikes and appear in July and August. They may be either single or double. The doubles seed just as freely as the singles, but after several years they will revert to single-flowered types.

It is perhaps easier, and certainly less expensive, to start a Hollyhock planting from seeds, but most all the varieties are obtainable as started plants from the usual mail order sources.

A. rosea — single-flowered forms — The following sources list these in a mixture of colors including red, pink, apricot, copper, yellow and white, etc.
Sources: 3,39,68,69; E

Hollyhock leaves disfigured by Japanese Beetles and Hollyhock Rust disease.

A. rosea — double forms — The following sources list these in separate colors.
Sources: 28,46,66; C,E,F,J

A. rosea — double forms — The following sources list these in a mixture of colors
Sources: 24,25,28,30,60,69; C,I

The following are named strains or cultivars, all having double flowers:

A. rosea 'Chaters Double' — Full range of colors. Chaters Hybrids also include single-flowered forms, but they seldom are available from nurseries.
Sources: 14,23,58,68; A,B,E,K,L

A. rosea 'Newport Pink' — Double pink flowers.
Sources: 24,60; E,I

***A. rosea* 'Pompadour'** — Another double strain including all the range of colors. Petals tend to be crinkled, with a single row of outer petals surrounding the usual double "half-ball" of petals.
Source: 67

***A. rosea* 'Powderpuff Hybrids'** — Very double flowers, often with longer flower spikes than the 'Chaters Double' forms.
Sources: 3,14,24,28,68,69; A,I

Alyssum saxatile   **Basket-of-Gold, Goldentuft Alyssum, Madwort**
Mustard Family (Cruciferae)
Commonly seen in rock gardens displaying its bright yellow blossoms on 12-inch stems in April or early May, Goldentuft Alyssum can be recommended for low maintenance borders only if the soil is dry and approximates rock garden conditions. Plants assume a coarse, sprawling habit in response to rich or moist soils, or shady conditions. It is best to encourage new growth by cutting back the stems to about half their length after flowering. If *Alyssum saxatile* is to be used in the herbaceous border, the two compact varieties discussed below should be given preference. They are best seen at the very front of the garden in groups of two or three planted 10 to 12 inches apart.
Sources: 14,23,37,39,46,54,67

***A. saxatile* 'Citrinum'** — Flowers lemon-yellow, contrasting well with the silvery leaves.
Sources: 3,13,66,69; B,C,J,K

***A. saxatile* 'Compactum'** — Neater, slower growing than the species, and will not require division for a number of years. Flowers the same bright yellow as the species, contrasting well with the silver foliage.
Sources: 3,13,66,67,68,69; A,B,C,J,K,L

***A. saxatile* 'Compactum Flora-plena'** (frequently listed as *A. saxatile* 'Flora Plena') — Double-flowered compact form; flowers brighter yellow than the preceding cultivar, but not produced as freely as in the species.
Sources: 13,32,66,67,69; C

***A. saxatile* 'Silver Queen'** — Lemon-yellow flowers which are most attractive against the silvery leaves.
Source: 68

Althaea rosea — *The single form of Hollyhock growing in a nearly wild state at the far side of Bussey Hill in the Arnold Arboretum. Photo: P. Bruns.*

Amsonia tabernaemontana   Amsonia, Willow Amsonia
                                 Dogbane Family (Apocynaceae)

An American plant native from Pennsylvania to Florida and Texas, this has been neglected by gardeners and yet is one of the easiest plants to grow.

Amsonia is very hardy, insect and disease-resistant, slow-growing and never invasive. It does almost equally well in moist or dry soils, is easily transplanted in spring or fall, never needs staking, does well in full sun or partial shade (perhaps a little better with some shade), and the foliage remains in excellent condition throughout the growing season. The tough stems are quite resistant to wind and the plant will thrive in seaside gardens.

Few plants possess so many virtues, so perhaps Amsonia may be excused if it is not the showiest plant in the border when in blossom. The clusters of small star-shaped flowers appear for two weeks at the end of May and into June and are an attractive steel-blue color, quite unlike the blue of any other perennial except some varieties of *Echinops*.

Plants grow to a height of 2 to 3 feet and form clumps about 1½ to 2 feet wide. Because they do not produce a great show of color, they are best seen as single specimens or small groups near the front or toward the middle of the border. Clumps remain in good condition for many years so division, except for purposes of increase, is unnecessary. Another native species, *A. salicifolia*, is quite similar in appearance and also may be in the trade listed as *A. tabernaemontana*.

Sources: 1,3,24,49,57,66,69; I

(Source number 66 lists an early and a late flowering form as well as the species.)

A. ciliata — Even less frequently grown than *A. tabernaemontana*, but equally worthy. Much lower growing, to 18 inches.
Source: 50

Anaphalis yedoensis   Japanese Pearly Everlasting
                               Daisy Family (Compositae)

This is a close relative of our own native *A. margaritacea*, but more suitable for the perennial garden. The pearly white, button-like flowers are profusely borne in clusters 2 inches wide on 2-foot stems. They are conspicuous from mid-July until

September, and both the flowers and silver foliage are excellent for cutting and drying. Plants are of a compact, bushy habit. They will grow in any well-drained soil in full sun, and are particularly useful in hot or dry areas. Best at the front of the garden, they will hold their own as single specimens or in groups of three planted about 10 inches apart. Division usually is required after the fourth year.
Sources: 24,67; I

Anchusa azurea (syn. *A. italica*)   Italian Alkanet, Italian Bugloss
Borage Family (Boraginaceae)
Beautiful but demanding, some plants are best admired in other people's gardens; perhaps Italian Bugloss is such a plant. It blooms for a long period and has flowers of true-blue, a color which is always welcome. Not particular as to soil, it must be well watered in periods of drought. Plants grow from 4 to 6 feet tall and require no staking, but are coarse and bristly; after flowering, the foliage becomes very unattractive. A secondary, lesser blooming period is encouraged if the plants are cut back. They invariably start to deteriorate after the second year (sometimes the first), and must be divided. They also have a very bad habit of seeding in all over; a distinct nuisance, especially if the garden is small.
Source: 66

The following varieties all require frequent division and are equally prone to seeding in:

A. *azurea* **'Little John'** — Lowest growing variety, about 1 to 1½ feet; deep blue flowers.
Sources: 24,69; I

A. *azurea* **'Loddon Royalist'** — Another good blue variety. Not over 3 feet.
Sources: 66,67

A. *azurea* **'Pride of Dover'** — Flowers medium blue. Unlike the others requires staking; height 4 feet.
Source: 69

A. *azurea* **'Royal Blue'** (also listed as 'Dropmore Royal Blue') — Smaller in stature; to 3 feet. Large deep gentian-blue flowers.
Sources: 13,24,69; C,I

Anchusa mysotidiflora — This is the old name for a most valuable garden plant; it still is listed this way in most catalogs. See *Brunnera macrophylla*.

Anemone × hybrida *cultivar*

Anemone × *hybrida*   **Japanese Anemone**
                          Buttercup Family (Ranunculaceae)

Anemones are a large garden group. Some belong in the general category of bulbous plants; others are for rock or wildflower gardens. The varieties of *A.* × *hybrida* (mainly *A. hupehensis* var. *japonica* selections) and one variety of *A. vitifolia* — the Grape-leaved Anemone — are of interest in this discussion. We hesitate to give them unqualified approval, for in our area they will not be hardy if the proper circumstances cannot be provided. If they can, these Anemones will reward the gardener for many years without much further attention. So, although most of the group cannot be recommended for low maintenance situations, we would suggest that you try a plant or two if your conditions approximate those described. If you succeed for three years, you ought to try more.

Anemones require a rich soil well supplied with humus, but it must be very well drained. Partial shade is recommended for best performance but plants will often tolerate exposure to full sun. If the soil dries out in summer, irrigation should be provided. The worst enemy in winter is an overly wet soil; this, more than anything else, will lessen the plants' ability to survive the dormant season. In the Boston area, a winter mulch of straw, oak leaves, or evergreen boughs is advisable, but not until the ground is thoroughly frozen. Set out potted plants in the spring so they will have sufficient time to become established before winter.

The Japanese and Grape-leaved Anemones blossom in white or shades of pink from late summer to mid-autumn. The handsome dark green leaves are deeply lobed and on established specimens form dense mounds up to 2 feet wide. The flowering stems reach a height of 2 to 3 feet depending upon variety. The plants increase slowly in size and require several years to form full-sized clumps. When circumstances are to their liking, they will remain in good condition for many years and dislike being disturbed. Best seen in groups of three, they may be planted about 1½ feet apart.

A. × *hybrida* '**Alba**' — Single white flowers 2 to 3 inches across, with only one ring of petals.
Sources: 13,24,32,66,67,68; B,C,I

A. × *hybrida* '**Max Vogel**' — Semidouble, rose-pink.
Sources: 24; I

A. × *hybrida* '**Prince Henry**' — Large double, deep purplish-pink.
Source: 32

A. × *hybrida* '**Profusion**' — Semidouble deep rose-pink. Plants somewhat dwarf, about 2 feet.
Source: 67

A. × *hybrida* '**Queen Charlotte**' — Semidouble deep pink.
Sources: 24,32,58,66; I

A. × *Hybrida* 'September Charm' — Single silvery-pink shaded rose-mauve.
Sources: 13,24,32,66,67; B,C,I

A. × *hybrida* 'September Sprite' — Single rose-pink.
Sources: 13; C

A. × *hybrida* 'Whirlwind' — Semidouble white.
Sources: 13,32,66,68; C

A. hupehensis var. *japonica* — Flowers rose-pink to purple.
Sources: 66,68

Anemone pulsatilla (or, properly, *Pulsatilla vulgaris*) — Pasque Flower — Listed by many suppliers of perennials, but is better suited to the rock garden).

A. vitifolia 'Robustissima' — Grape-leaved Anemone — This is the hardiest of the autumn Anemones. Plants have survived in the Low Maintenance Garden of the Arnold Arboretum with only minimal winter protection and where the soil was too moist for other varieties. Very similar in appearance to the Japanese types and very free-blooming with light pink flowers.
Sources: 13,24,66,67; C,I

Antennaria   Pussytoes, Cat's-Ear
                                            Daisy Family (Compositae)
Diminutive plants of the Daisy family, well-suited to the rock garden or for planting between paving stones; however, of little value in the perennial border.

Anthemis tinctoria
                            Golden Marguerite, Golden or Ox-Eye Camomile
                                            Daisy Family (Compositae)
Unfortunately, this plant and its several cultivars cannot be considered for low maintenance situations. They require division every other year or clumps will tend to develop a dead area in the center. Most all varieties require staking as well; otherwise, this is a fine plant for hot, dry areas with sandy soil where most other plants fail. In such situations it will thrive and produce masses of flowers in July, continuing until September if the faded blossoms are removed. The yellow flowers are Daisy-like and make excellent subjects for cutting; the leaves are aromatic. Golden Marguerite grows to about 2½ feet.
Sources: 46; E

A. *tinctoria* 'Beauty of Grallagh' — Deep golden-yellow flowers on bushy, 2½ to 3-foot plants.
Source: 32

A. *tinctoria* 'E. C. Buxton' — Lemon-yellow flowers. 2½ feet.
Source: 32

A. *tinctoria* 'Kelwayi' — Deep yellow. 2 feet.
Sources: 68,69; B,J,L

A. *tinctoria* 'Moonlight' — Pale yellow.
Sources: 13,24,32,57,58,66,67; C,I

Other types offered:

A. *biebersteiniana* — Flowers bright yellow. Best as a rock garden plant. 10 to 12 inches.
Sources: 66,68

A. *sancti-johannis* — St. John's Camomile. — Flowers 1½ to 2 inches across, bright orange. Same uses as *A. tinctoria*. 2½ feet.
Source: B

Aquilegia   Columbine
                                  Buttercup Family (Ranunculaceae)
Unless one can provide excellent drainage, Columbines are apt to be transitory in nature and of no value to those who have little time to continuously replace plants. We cannot disregard them altogether, though, for if they find conditions to their liking, they seed in on their own and seedlings in unwanted places are not difficult to control. Many of the popular long-spurred cultivars possess a decided tendency to degenerate into all sorts of "mongrels" when seeding occurs.

Columbines have another bad feature which must be taken into consideration if space is limited. Often they suffer from leaf miners, insects which eat their way through the tissues of the leaves and produce characteristic "tunnels." These pests are difficult to control, and when the flowers are gone, one is left with a not-too-beautiful display of debilitated foliage.

There are a large number of species and cultivated strains from which to choose. The Alpine sorts are difficult and should be avoided by the novice. A. 'Mrs. Scott Elliot' and A. 'McKanna's Giants' are old favorites of vigorous growth and fairly easy culture.

Flowers appear in late May and June, and, depending upon variety, are between 1½ to 4 inches across, mainly in shades of red, yellow, pink, white, blue, or lavender. The sepals, which surround the five true petals (arranged like a cup), may be the same color, or contrast in color, to the petals. A spur varying in length from ½-inch to 6 inches is attached to the back of each petal. Culture is fairly simple. As mentioned above, good drainage is a necessity, but plants will not tolerate an overly dry soil.

Leaves of Columbine marred by leaf miners.

Either full sun or light shade is satisfactory, but a shady condition will prolong the flowering season somewhat. Leaf miner can be controlled to some degree by spraying with Malathion in early and mid-May; however, we recommend that all affected plants be removed and burned.

A selection of the many varieties available includes:

A. chrysantha — Golden Columbine — Native to the Rocky Mountains and the Southwest. Shades of yellow. Long spurs. Flowers 2 to 3 inches across. Plants 3 feet high.
Sources: 3,24,46,68,69; I,L

A. chrysantha 'Silver Queen' — A white-flowered selection of the above. Flowering season is longer than most of the others.
Sources: 3,69

A. coerulea — Colorado Columbine — Another species native to the Rocky Mountains; the State Flower of Colorado. Blue sepals,

creamy-white petals, slender spurs 1½ inches long. Plants 2½ feet tall. Quite short-lived in hot locations.
Sources: 3,24; I

A. flabellata — Fan Columbine — From Japan. White flowers tinged with lavender-rose in late April, and light green foliage. 15 inches high.
Source: 4

A. flabellata 'Nana Alba' — Good dwarf form of the above with pure white flowers. 6 inches high and suited to the very front of the border. Frequently used in rock gardens.
Sources: 3,4,68

A. 'Copper Queen' — Flowers copper-red.
Sources: 24; I

A. 'Crimson Star' — Petals white, tinged with red. Long crimson-red sepals and spurs.
Sources: 3,4,24,32,37,68,69; I,K,L

A. 'Dragonfly Hybrids' — Includes the normal range of colors. Flowers are long-spurred. Plants semidwarf, to 18 inches.
Sources: 4,24,68; B,E,I,K

A. 'McKanna's Giant Hybrids' — The most popular strain. An All-American Seed Trial winner in 1955. Extensive color range, very sturdy growth. The large flowers have spurs 4 inches and more long. 2½ to 3 feet tall.
Sources: 4,13,14,23,24,25,28,30,32,37,46,53,58,66,68,69; A,B,C, E,F,G,I,J,K,L

A. 'Mrs. Scott Elliot Hybrids' — Now of somewhat lesser value than the preceding, but used to be the standard varieties. Flowers somewhat smaller, but the colors tend to be deeper and range through shades of crimson, purple, blue, and pink. 2½ to 3 feet tall.
Sources: 25,53; J,L

A. 'Rose Queen' — Pure white petals, rose-colored sepals.
Sources: 3,32,37,69; K,L

Arabis 　　　　　　　　　　　Rock Cress, Wall Cress
　　　　　　　　　　Mustard Family (Cruciferae)
　　Many types offered by dealers in perennials, but best suited to hot dry areas in rock gardens.

Arenaria 　　　　　　　　　　　　　　　Sandwort
　　　　　　　Carnation Family (Coryophyllaceae)
　　Mat-forming plants, some almost mosslike in appearance. Best suited to the rock garden; sometimes used as ground covers.

Armeria   **Thrift, Sea-Pink**
                              Leadwort Family (Plumbaginaceae)
Most members of this group are traditional rock garden subjects, but they may also be of value at the very front of the
border if the proper soil conditions can be provided. They all
possess neat, compact tufts of evergreen foliage. _A. maritima_
and its cultivars are very low-growing, mat-forming plants useful where the soil is poor and dry. Rich or overly moist soil
conditions will cause the mats to rot at the centers and become
unsightly after about the second year. The varieties of _A. planta-
ginea_ and _A. pseudoarmeria_ are taller, to 2 feet, and find suitable
positions a bit further back from the front. All have globular
heads of flowers. The basic shade is pink; some are intense
pink. All varieties may be left in place until the clumps begin
to deteriorate, normally after the fourth year. They all should
be given a position in full sun with sharp drainage at the roots.

A. _maritima_ — Sea-Pink, Common Thrift — Forms dense, rounded mats 3 to 4 inches tall, about 1½ feet wide, and has blossom
stems up to 10 inches. Flowers light pink to rose-pink; the species is somewhat variable.
Sources: 14,68

A. _maritima_ var. _alba_ — The white-flowered form of the above
species. It is considered quite choice.
Sources: 24,66,67,69; I

A. _maritima_ 'Brilliant' — Bright pink.
Sources: 32,66

A. _maritima_ 'Laucheana' — Plants very tufted, to 6 inches tall.
Flowers intense rose-pink in dense heads.
Sources: 13,24,39,66,67,69; B,C,I,J,L

A. _maritima_ 'Vindictive' — Deep rosy-red.
Sources: 24; I

A. _plantaginea_ 'Bee's Ruby' — Cultivar of Plantain Thrift —
Taller, to 1½ to 2 feet when in flower. Blossoms bright ruby-red
in June and July. Effective when massed as a group of three or
more planted about a foot apart.
Sources: 13,24,66; C,I

A. _pseudoarmeria_ 'Glory of Holland' — Cultivar of Giant or Pink-
ball Thrift (usually listed under the old species name _A. cephal-_

Armeria maritima — *At the very front of the border, this five-year-old speci-men has been effectively combined with Coral Bells and Peonies.*

otes) — To 2 feet when in blossom. Flower heads large, deep pink.
Sources: A,J,K,L

A. 'Royal Rose' — Rich pink flowers on 15-inch stems.
Source: 67

Artemisia   **Artemisia, Wormwood, Mugwort**
                                Daisy Family (Compositae)
Silver or gray foliage can be used in the perennial border in a number of ways, either to provide notes of accent or as a contrast to such colors as blue, red, pink, or yellow.

In our area, for really reliable gray foliage plants, we must depend upon the Artemisias. Even of this large group, for low maintenance situations we can recommend only two: one short, and one tall. In addition to the gray foliage, all of the group have finely divided aromatic foliage. Flowers are yellowish or white, and insignificant for the most part. The plants perform best in light, well-drained soils, even infertile ones; all should be planted in full sun.

A. abrotanum — Southernwood, Old Man — This is actually a slender shrub since the stems are woody. It grows from 3 to 5 feet tall depending on the fertility of the soil and is suited to the middle or rear of the border. The leaves are grayish-green, much divided and pleasantly aromatic. Plant Southernwood singly or, for strong accents, in groups of three, about 1½ feet apart. Division is not necessary, but cutting back from time to time may be required to keep plants vigorous.
Sources: 13,24,32,39,46,69; C,I

A. schmidtiana 'Silver Mound' — Angels Hair — This has become one of the most popular plants listed in catalogs of perennials. It grows to a height of 12 inches and forms a rounded mound about 1½ feet in diameter. The bright silvery foliage is of the greatest value in border foregrounds. If A. 'Silver Mound' is planted in too rich a soil, growth is lush and the mound of foliage flops and opens in the center; therefore, it would be best to use this plant where hot, sunny conditions prevail and soil conditions are relatively poor.
Sources: 3,13,14,20,24,25,28,30,39,46,49,58,59,66,67,68,69; A, B,C,G,H,I,J,K,L

All the following are of value in our area when silver-foliaged plants are needed. They require frequent division, usually on an annual basis, or some will deteriorate and others will become invasive.

A. absinthicum — Wormwood — 2 to 4 feet tall. Leaves white and silky. Spreads quickly.
Sources: 13,24,39; C,I

A. albula 'Silver King' (frequently listed in catalogs as 'Silver King,' rather than by the species name) — Ghost plant — 2 to 3 feet tall. Silvery-gray leaves.
Sources: 13,14,24,25,32,39,59,66,67,68; B,C,I,K,L

A. albula 'Silver Queen' — Similar to the preceding, but the leaves are more glistening, intense silver.
Source: 66

Artemisia schmidtiana 'Silver Mound' — *The distinctive shape and finely textured foliage (shown below) can be used for effective accents in front of taller growing perennials or shrubs.*

A. frigida — Fringed Sagewort — Silvery leaves, deeply cut. 8 to 12 inches tall.
Sources: 13,32,49; A,C

A. lactiflora — White Mugwort — 4 feet tall. Fine-textured leaves. About the only Artemisia valued for its flowers which are creamy-white in August and September.
Sources: 13,24,32,49; C,I

A. stelleriana — Beach Wormwood, Dunesilver, Dusty Miller, Old Woman — Native along our coast. Beautiful silvery-white leaves. Plants about 2 feet tall.
Sources: 13,14,24,32,46,66,68,69; C,I

Aruncus sylvester   Goats-Beard
                                          Rose Family (Rosaceae)
This is a very desirable subject for the rear of the border, especially in low maintenance situations, and it is strange that it is so infrequently offered by nurserymen. Resembling a giant Astilbe, its attractive compound foliage is topped with large, showy plumes of white flowers in mid-June. We emphasize that this is a large plant. It grows to 5 feet tall with a spread of over 3 feet; but despite the height, staking is not required. Tolerant of a wide range of soil conditions, it can be grown almost anywhere. In situations away from the border, Goats-Beard could compete with shrubbery in the landscape. It deserves to be more popular.
Sources: 29,66

A. sylvester 'Kneiffii' — Similar to the species except that it has more finely-cut foliage and is therefore more graceful in appearance. Unfortunately we are unable to locate a mail-order source.
Source: 66

Asclepias tuberosa   Butterfly Weed, Pleurisy Root
                        Milkweed Family (Asclepiadaceae)
This should be tried in every garden where the soil is poor or sandy and dry, particularly if a place in full sun can be given. This native American is hardy and showy in flower, has a long life, will never outgrow its allotted space, has no insect or disease problems, and once established requires almost no attention. This is the type of description we immediately suspect as

Asclepias tuberosa — *Butterfly Weed*

[38]

"phony" in advertisements for some plants, but if you do not encourage Butterfly Weed with a rich or moist soil, excellent results should be expected.

It grows from 2 to 3 feet tall with hairy stems and leaves which are pointed. The orange flowers in midsummer are borne in umbels and last for about two weeks. They are followed by the typical Milkweed-type pods which are attractive in dried arrangements.

Butterfly Weed develops a tap root, so once established it is very difficult to move. Young potted plants obtained from nurseries may be planted either in the spring or autumn. They are slow to start in the spring so careful cultivation will be necessary until the new growths appear; division is not recommended.

Sources: 1,3,5,7,13,14,24,25,27,29,30,39,46,57,58,60,66,67,68, 69; A,B,C,I,J,K,L

Aster   Hardy Aster, Michaelmas Daisy, Starwort
                                       Daisy Family (Compositae)

The requirement of annual division for some, and every other year for most of the rest, removes this large and valuable group from most low maintenance borders — even though the plants are easy to grow otherwise. Because Asters are of great value from late summer to late autumn, and particularly because they are much easier than Chrysanthemums, many gardeners certainly will wish to have a few varieties. Long admired in Europe, particularly in Britain, Asters have not always been as popular here — probably because the parents are common "weeds" along our roadsides. In fact, *A. novae-angliae* the New England Aster, *A. novae-belgii*, the New York Aster, and *A. ericoides*, the Heath Aster are the principal parents of the modern cultivars, although a few other species are involved.

Apart from frequent division, culture is fairly simple: spring is the best time for planting; full sun and a well-drained, light soil are best; ordinary fertility will do. In humid summers, the leaves of some cultivars are susceptible to mildew and rust diseases. Height, according to variety, ranges from under a foot to about 6 feet. Those over 2 feet may require staking. This is best done in the European manner by placing twiggy branches 2½ to 3 feet high (4 feet for the taller sorts) amongst the plants while the growth is still low. As the plants grow, these twigs will provide support, but will be largely hidden by the foliage.

The following is but a sampling of the many varieties available:

A. 'Autumn Glory' — Rich red. 3½ to 4 feet tall.
Sources: 13,67; C

A. 'Countess of Dudley' — Clear pink. 9 to 12 inches tall. September.
Sources: 68; K

A. 'Crimson Brocade' — Crimson-red. 3 feet tall.
Sources: 24,59,67,69; I

A. 'Eventide' — Deep violet-blue. 3½ feet tall.
Sources: 3,13,28,32,58,59,66,67,68,69; C,H,K

A. 'Finalist' — Strong violet-blue. 2½ to 3 feet tall. Very late flowering, October to mid-November.
Source: 67

A. × *frikartii* 'Wonder of Stäfa'(usually listed as *A. frikartii* [sic.], this is a hybrid between *A. thomsonii* and *A. amellus*) — Bears lavender-blue flowers from July to October, even during periods of drought. In our area frequently requires the protection of a winter mulch to be hardy, especially if the soil is at all wet; usually needs staking too.
Sources: 3,13,14,24,32,44,58,59,60,66,67,68,69; B,C,G,I

A. 'Harrington's Pink' — Pure pink; mid-September blooming. 4 feet tall. Requires less frequent division; probably would be one of the best for a low maintenance situation.
Sources: 3,13,24,59,66,68,69; B,C,I,L

A. 'Patricia Ballard' — Fully double, pink; when flowers are young has a yellow "eye" in the center as do the other varieties. 3 feet tall. September to October.
Sources: 32,59,67,68,69; H,K

A. 'Violetta' — Rich deep blue. 2 to 3 feet tall with a rounded habit. September.
Sources: 67,68

A. 'White Lady' — Good pure white. 2 to 3 feet tall. September to October.
Source: 68

A. 'Ypres' — Rosy-pink. 1½ feet tall. September.
Source: 68

Astilbe   **Astilbe, False Spiraea, False Goat's Beard**
                   Saxifrage Family (Saxifragaceae)
Astilbes have become an almost indispensable feature of waterside plantings, and thrive where soils are rich and moist in the summer. Their main enemy, however, is a wet soil in winter. The plants are heavy feeders and exhaust the soil around them, hence they may need to be divided at frequent intervals (every three years) if maximum flowering is to be ob-

tained. The roots are shallow so at planting time it is not necessary to re-work the soil deeply, but ample amounts of fertilizer and organic matter should be added.

In a low maintenance situation, Astilbes may remain for much longer than three years before they are divided. The flower spikes will not be as large, or the plants as vigorous, but an acceptable display still can be had, especially if they receive a top dressing of a 5–10–10 fertilizer each spring. Best in partial shade, the plants may be situated in full sun if the soil does not dry out easily.

The flowers themselves are very small, but are displayed in June and July in dense, erect or arching panicles about 2 feet tall. There is a wide range of colors, often in vivid pastel hues, from purple to red, pink, or white. Foliage ranges in color from green to bronzy green and is dissected and decidedly attractive. Many of the cultivars are classified under the general name *A. × arendsii* and result from the breeding efforts of George Arends of Ronsdorf, Germany, who crossed several species and produced a dazzling array of colors.

The following is but a selection of the many available types:

A. 'Avalanche' — White. 18 inches. Deeply cut, dark green foliage.
Sources: 24,32,69; I,L

A. chinensis var. pumila — Dwarf Chinese Astilbe — Very dwarf, only 6 to 8 inches. Unlike the others, has a creeping habit and blooms in August. Flowers lavender-pink.
Sources: 13,32,49,66; C

A. 'Deutschland' — Pure white. 24 inches.
Sources: 24,58,66,67,68,69; B,I,L

A. 'Europa' — Clear pink. 1½ to 2 feet. Foliage dark green.
Sources: 66,68,69; B

A. 'Fanal' — Deep garnet-red. 1½ feet. Foliage dark reddish-green.
Sources: 13,23,25,58,66,68,69; C,L

A. 'Irrlicht' — Pure white. 1½ to 2 feet.
Sources: 13,49,66,68; C

A. 'Mainz' — Deep rose. 18 to 20 inches.
Sources: 24,49,68; I,J

Astilbe $\times$ arendsii *'Deutschland'*. *Photo: P. Bruns.*

A. 'Montgomery' — Deep red. 2 feet.
Sources: 20,24,49,66; B,I,L

A. 'Peach Blossom' — Pale peach-pink. 30 inches.
Sources: 13,24,25,58,66,68,69; C,I,L

A. 'Queen Alexandra' — Soft rose. 2 to 2½ feet.
Sources: 3,49,68; L

A. 'Red Sentinel' — Rich, intense red. 2 feet.
Sources: 3,13,66,67,68,69; B,C,J,L

A. 'Rheinland' — Carmine-pink. 2 to 2½ feet.
Sources: 24,32,67,69; B,I,J,L

Baptisia australis   **Blue or False Indigo**
Pea Family (Leguminosae)

It has been suggested that our native *B. australis* might be desirable for those who have difficulties with Delphiniums and Lupines. If grown specifically for this purpose, it may prove to be a rather poor substitute; but the plant is of value in many other ways.

It does not require a rich soil, has no serious insect or disease problems, will live on for a number of years in one spot, and will not become invasive. It is tolerant of full sun or partial shade. The indigo-blue flowers are borne in terminal racemes on stems 3 to 4 feet in height. After flowering in June, attractive inflated black pods develop which are as handsome on the plants as they are in dried arrangements. *Baptisia australis* is also a member of that group whose foliage remains in good condition all summer. Although the plants are tall and suited to the middle or rear of the border, they will not require staking. One author has suggested that this may be just the plant for the person who says, "I can't grow a single thing."
Sources: 3,4,13,24,45,46,58,66,67,68,69; C,I

Belamcanda chinensis   **Blackberry Lily, Leopard Flower**
Iris Family (Iridaceae)

Often described as not reliably hardy in colder regions, this somewhat unusual member of the Iris clan is perfectly hardy in Boston in our experience; in fact it has escaped and formed colonies in the wild in some parts of New England. In Western Massachusetts or northern New England it will require the protection of a mulch in winter. This plant seems to have been much more popular in bygone days; it deserves a comeback.

Out of flower, the plant resembles a large Iris, about 3 feet in height. The flat, star-shaped, 2-inch flowers are orange spotted with red, an exotic combination for northern gardens. They appear in late July and August on stems 3 to 4 feet tall. Also interesting are the shiny black clusters of seeds which somewhat resemble a raspberry in shape and appear after the seed pods burst. These persist for a long time and are useful in winter dried arrangements. Self-seeding may occur, but young plants are easily removed if not wanted.

Culture is simple. A place in the sun and well-drained soil are about the only requirements; soggy soil conditions in winter may prove fatal. About the only insect problem is caused by the Iris Borer which may occasionally attack the fleshy rhizomes. For control, see *Iris*. Blackberry Lilies do not lend themselves well to mass effects; they are seen best as single specimens placed somewhere between the front and the middle of the border. Division will not be necessary for a number of years.
Sources: 1,4,25,27,39,58,69; B

Bergenia   **Bergenia, Megasea, Pig Squeak**
Saxifrage Family (Saxifragaceae)
Bergenias have uses in many garden situations due to their tolerance of a wide variety of conditions: sun or shade, moist or dry soil, which either can be moderately rich or moderately poor. They are recommended most frequently for use in rock gardens, along stream banks, or as ground covers for small areas. They are low plants, not over a foot in height, so their use in a perennial garden would be restricted to the very front. Where perennials are displayed in combination with shrubbery, Bergenias can be very useful as edging. They are prized for the glossy green, 8 to 10-inch, rounded, cabbage-like leaves which are evergreen with reddish tints in the winter. The flowers are of secondary interest; in our area they may not be produced after a severe winter or if the plants are in exposed locations. The flowers are borne on short stems just above the foliage and, depending on variety, are pink, rose-pink, or white.

Little care is necessary. If the soil is a dry one, plants can

Bergenia cordifolia — *Heartleaf Bergenia*

go for many years before they will require division; but this may be necessary after about the third or fourth year if plants are encouraged into excessive growth by very fertile soil conditions. They spread by rhizomes on the surface of the ground; as these grow away from the center and the clumps expand, bare spots may result. Division, leaving a short piece of the rhizome (3 to 4 inches is enough), is best done in the spring so that the new plants will have the benefit of a growing season to produce new roots and become established by winter. Single specimens appear lonely, so plant several in a group about 1 foot apart.

B. cordifolia — Heartleaf Bergenia — Very hardy, the most commonly-planted species. Leaves are rounded, somewhat heart-shaped and toothed at the margins. Flowers reddish-pink. Sources: 13,32,59,66,67,68,69; B,C,J

B. cordifolia* var. *purpurea — Flowers purplish-pink.
Source: 66

B. crassifolia — Leather Bergenia — Less commonly grown in our area. Leaves more oval than round. Flowers reddish-pink.
Source: 32

B. crassifolia* var. *orbicularis — Leaves broader than the preceding. Flowers pink.
Sources: 66,68
We have not tried some of the other species and interesting hybrids offered by a few nurserymen on the West Coast, so are unprepared to comment on their hardiness.

Betonica grandiflora — See *Stachys grandiflora*

Boltonia	**Boltonia, False Camomile, False Starwort**
	Daisy Family (Compositae)

Similar in appearance to, but taller than, most of the Fall Asters, they have a much more limited range of flower colors. Culture is the same. Division is required annually or every other year. Staking is mandatory.

B. asteroides — Grows to about 6 feet high. Lilac or purple flowers.
Sources: 24,66,68; I

B. latisquama — Violet Boltonia — Grows to about 6 feet high. Flowers bluish-violet and showier than those of *B. asteroides*.
Sources: 4,46

Brunnera macrophylla	**Dwarf Anchusa, Siberian Bugloss**
	Borage Family (Boraginaceae)

A very easy plant to grow, especially in light shade where the soil is somewhat moist. In April to early June it is of value for the branched racemes of small, clear blue, starlike flowers similar to those of Anchusa or Forget-me-nots. Throughout the rest of the growing season the dark green 6 to 8-inch heart-shaped leaves provide an excellent foliage effect. The leaves increase in size from spring until midsummer, at which time they give the most effective display. Plants range in height

from about a foot to 18 inches and may be planted singly or in a group of three or more placed about 15 inches apart; they are suitable for use as a deciduous ground cover in a shady moist area. It will be many years before the clumps open at the center and require division.
Sources: 3,13,23,24,32,49,66,67,68,69; B,C,I,J,K,L

Campanula   **Bellflower**
Bellflower Family (Campanulaceae)
This is a large and varied group with many members which are of great value in the rock garden; some, in the perennial garden; and one which is such a pestiferous weed it never should be in any garden.

The principal sorts for the perennial garden have similar, easy cultural requirements. They will tolerate either full sun or partial shade. The soil should be well drained and need be of only average fertility. All are best seen in groups of about three rather than as single specimens. Under most conditions, staking of the taller varieties will not be necessary. Clumps need not be divided until deterioration starts; this will, in most cases, be about every four years. Spring rather than fall planting, is usually recommended. Removal of the seed heads will prolong the flowering and prevent undesirable self-seeding.

C. persicifolia (listed in some catalogs as C. *persicifolia* 'Grandiflora Coerulea') — Peach-leaved Bellflower, Peach Bells — We place this species and its cultivars first in value for the low maintenance garden. They grow to a height of 2 to 2½ feet and bloom in July. The several erect stems from the base of the plant bear a profusion of cup-shaped flowers in shades of blue or white and are excellent for cutting. It is said that the plants are best divided every other year, or every third year, to keep them vigorous; in our experience they can go for at least four years before this may be necessary. The species has light blue flowers.
Sources: 3,4,13,24,46,53,67,69; C,I,K

C. persicifolia var. **alba** (this is listed by some nurseries as 'Alba Grandiflora') — Same as the above, but the flowers are white.
Sources: 3,13,24,66,67,68,69; C,I,K

C. persicifolia 'Blue Gardenia' — Flowers deep silvery-blue, double.
Source: 32

Brunnera macrophylla — *Siberian Bugloss. Photo: P. Bruns.*

[49]

***C. persicifolia* 'Landham's Giants'** — Assortment of shades of blue and white.
Sources: 24; I

***C. persicifolia* 'Telham Beauty'** — Often considered one of the best, but may require more frequent division. Large, single, 3-inch porcelain-blue flowers.
Sources: 32,66,68; B

***C. persicifolia* 'White Pearl'** — Flowers white, double.
Sources: 24,32; I

C. glomerata — Clustered Bellflower, Danesblood — In a low maintenance situation these are recommended only for positions in full sun; in shade they spread rapidly by runners and will become invasive. Plants are 1½ to 2 feet tall and bloom in late spring and early summer. The flowers are borne in dense upward-facing clusters in shades of blue, purple, or white. Axillary flowers open after the terminal head has finished.

C. glomerata* var. *acaulis — The lowest-growing variety, not exceeding 8 inches. Quite large, purple flowers.
Sources: 13,66; C

***C. glomerata* 'Crown of Snow'** — Large white flowers in dense clusters.
Source: 69

***C. glomerata* 'Joan Elliott'** — Deep violet-blue flowers.
Sources: 24,67; I

C. glomerata* var. *superba — Large heads of deep violet flowers.
Sources: 13,66,69; C

C. lactiflora — Milky Bellflower — Of easiest culture. Blooms from late June to the beginning of August with large blue, 1-inch flowers on 3-foot stems. The species itself appears not to be widely available at present, but the cultivar which follows is excellent in every respect.

***C. lactiflora* 'Pritchards Variety'** — This includes a range of colors from pale to deep blue.
Source: 70

C. latifolia — Great Bellflower — Another excellent species. It is very showy in blossom, and produces terminal racemes of violet-colored flowers in June and July. Plants are many-stemmed, to a height of 3 feet.
Source: 66

C. latifolia 'Brantwood' — Flowers deep violet.
Sources: 24,67; I

C. latifolia 'Macrantha' — Bright purple flowers which are up to 2½ inches across. The plant is very showy and grows taller than other cultivars of this species.
Source: 68

> The following have merit in the rock garden, or are biennials; one is included as a warning. We cannot recommend them for general purposes in the perennial border, but occasionally the lower growing sorts may be of use at the very front.

C. carpatica — Carpathian Harebell, Carpathian Bellflower — Beloved by rock gardeners, this forms neat clumps of foliage less than 6 inches high. The 2-inch blue or white cuplike flowers on 6 to 8-inch stems appear over a long period in June and July. The species has blue flowers.
Sources: 3,4,13,24,46,67,68,69; B,C,I,K,L

C. carpatica var. *alba* — The white-flowered form of the species.
Sources: 3,49,66,67,68,68; B

C. carpatica 'China Doll' — Lavender flowers.
Sources: 13,24,69; A,C,I,J,K

C. carpatica 'Blue Carpet' — Deep blue flowers.
Sources: 32,66

C. medium var. *calycanthema* — The well known Cup and Saucer form of Canterbury Bells. A biennial, it requires replacement each year to keep a succession. Often raised from seed; some nurseries sell started plants.
Sources: 13,66; C,J,L

C. rapunculoides — Rover Bellflower, False Rampion — In our area this is one of the most noxious weeds that can invade a garden. Although rather handsome in flower, it spreads freely and has become widely naturalized. The roots are fleshy, and the smallest portion left behind in weeding is capable of regenerating new plants which take over large areas in a relatively short time. Once established, the Rover Bellflower is nearly impossible to eradicate without resorting to herbicides, a chancy business in a perennial garden. Although a few nurseries offer this species for naturalizing in wild gardens, it is better enjoyed in waste places where it belongs.

C. rotundifolia — Harebell, Bluebells of Scotland — A diminutive species, not much over 10 to 12 inches when in flower. Flowers are small, nodding, and bell-like. In the species they are blue.
Sources: 13,24,46,67,68,69; C,I

C. rotundifolia var. *alba* — The white-flowered form of the species.
Source: 69

Cassia marylandica   **Wild Senna**
                                          Pea Family (Leguminosae)
  Here is another infrequently used native American plant
which has great potential in the perennial border and is excellent for low maintenance situations. It blooms in August,
with a profusion of bright yellow flowers in 3-inch clusters, on
stems 3 to 4 feet tall. Some large border plants have a coarse
appearance, but Wild Senna is extremely fine-textured and the
compound leaves remain in attractive condition throughout the
season. If the plant did not bloom at all, it still would be valuable on this account.
  Plants will grow for many years before division is necessary;
it is easily accomplished in early spring. Positions in either full
sun or partial shade are equally satisfactory, but wet soil conditions should be avoided. There are no insect or disease problems; staking is never necessary. When grown in a perennial
border, Wild Senna should be placed well to the rear. It is unfortunate that sources of supply are so limited.
Sources: 24; I

Catananche coerulea   **Cupid's Dart, Cupid's Love Dart**
                                          Daisy Family (Compositae)
  These plants, particularly the named color selections, require
division every year or every other year in order to perpetuate the
form and prevent the numerous inferior self-sown seedlings from
taking over. Also, they are short-lived if not frequently divided.
A sunny position is demanded; soggy soil in winter is fatal and
even under the best of conditions hardiness cannot always be
assured. The flowers are a good blue with deeper blue centers,
and somewhat similar in appearance to, but smaller than, Wild
Chicory. The ends of the petals typically look as if they have
been cut off with pinking shears. The leaves are silvery-green;
the flowers are excellent for cutting and drying. Of rather frail
habit, plants must be massed in groups of three, or preferably
more, to get a good effect. Flower stems reach a height of about
2 feet.
Sources: 3,13,14,24,66,69; C,I,K,L

C. coerulea var. alba — Silvery-white flowers.
Source: 69

C. coerulea 'Blue Giant' — Pale blue flowers.
Source: 67

Centaurea   **Daisy Family (Compositae)**

This group will survive all sorts of neglect if the right conditions can be given: a sunny aspect, and soil of ordinary fertility which is well drained, especially in winter. All plants of this group can endure considerable drought. With one exception, they can go four years or longer before division will be necessary. Spring planting is usually recommended. They all are very hardy.

C. dealbata — Persian Centaurea — Lilac to purple, deeply fringed flowers in mid-July and August, sometimes into autumn. The foliage is more finely textured than most other Centaureas, and somewhat white below. Best seen in groups of three, planted about a foot apart. 2 feet tall.
Sources: 13,24; C,I,K,L

C. dealbata 'Sternbergii' — Superior to the above. Petals are deeply notched and bright purple, surrounding clear white centers. Plants are quite bushy and blossom from the end of June into September.
Sources: 13; C

C. macrocephala — Globe Centaurea, Yellow-Hardhead — Grows to 3 to 4 feet and is considered to be coarse in appearance, partly because of the large, stiff leaves which are borne sparingly. The golden-yellow flowers appear in 3-inch Thistle-like heads in June and July. Best seen toward the middle or rear of the garden alone rather than in groups, this is a plant to consider when a bold effect may be wanted.
Sources: 13,24,58,67; C,E,I,J

C. ruthenica — Ruthenian Centaurea — Grows to 3 feet and is yellow-flowered, but not as coarse in appearance as the above. The leaves are deeply lobed, giving a somewhat finer-textured appearance.
Sources: 24; I

C. montana — Mountain Bluet or Knapweed, Hardy Bachelor's Button, Perennial Corn Flower — The most popular of the group, but requires division every other year or it will spread rapidly and become unkempt in appearance. Its tendency to self-sow can be a nuisance in some circumstances. Deep Corn-flower-blue flowers, 2 to 3 inches wide, on 2-foot stems.
Sources: 3,13,14,24,46,67,68; B,C,E,I,J,K,L

Centaurea montana — *Mountain Bluet*

Cerastium   **Snow-in-summer, Starry Grasswort**
Carnation Family (Caryophyllaceae)
Of great value for their handsome silver foliage, these plants spread rapidly; annual division will be necessary to keep them in check on all but the very poorest or driest soils. Best left to dry, exposed situations in the rock garden where they can romp; or to the top of walls which are set against banks of soil.

C. biebersteinii — Taurus Cerastium — Considered the choicest species; its spreading is not as offensive as the *C. tomentosum* clan. Silvery-gray leaves and white flowers which are larger than those of *C. tomentosum.*
Sources: 24; I

C. tomentosum — Snow-in-summer — 2-foot creeping stems, very silvery foliage. Covered with white flowers in June. Highly invasive; may be difficult to eradicate when well established.
Sources: 14,46,68; A,B,J,L

Ceratostigma plumbaginoides — *Blue Leadwort*

[54]

***C. tomentosum* 'Columnae'** — A dwarf form of the above. Only 4 to 6 inches tall.
Sources: 13; C,K

***C. tomentosum* 'Silver Carpet'** — Another dwarf selection. 6 inches tall.
Source: 67

Ceratostigma plumbaginoides **Blue Leadwort**
Leadwort Family (Plumbaginaceae)

The Latin name is quite a mouthful and this may account for the nearly universal use in catalogs of the old name *Plumbago larpentae*. This is a desirable little plant which produces an abundance of ½-inch blue flowers in late summer. Its maximum height is 6 to 8 inches, and when left undisturbed, plants form clumps 12 to 18 inches across. In fall the leaves turn a bronze-green and this color intensifies as the weather becomes cooler.

Blue Leadwort is not always reliably hardy in the Boston area, especially when soil conditions are wet in winter. A light covering with a winter mulch is advisable here, and mandatory further north.

Spring is the only planting time recommended. Plants are very late to appear in the spring and one may be fooled into thinking they have not survived the winter; thus early cultivation must be done with care and it may be wise to have some sort of a small marker to indicate the plants' location in a large garden.
Sources: 3,13,24,28,30,32,37,49,66,67,68,69,70; A,B,C,G,H,I,J,L

Chelone   **Turtlehead**

Figwort Family (Scrophulariaceae)

These are excellent plants for light shade where the soil is moist; they increase rapidly to form a large clump and division may be necessary by the fourth year. Otherwise, they are simple to grow and have no insect or disease problems. The maximum height is 3 to 4 feet. Best planted as single specimens instead of in a group because of their robust nature. Plants possess shiny dark green leaves, and the pink or white flowers are about an inch long in short terminal clusters appearing in August or September. The shape of the flower is supposed to resemble that of a turtle's head.

C. glabra — White Turtlehead, Snakehead — Flowers generally white, sometimes tinged with rose. 2 feet.
Sources: 39,43

C. lyoni — Pink Turtlehead — Flowers pink to rose-purple. 3 to 4 feet.
Sources: 39,46,68

C. obliqua — Rose Turtlehead — Flowers deep rose. 2 feet.
Sources: 29,66

Chelone lyoni — *Pink Turtlehead*

The soft rose-colored flowers of Chelone lyoni *combine well with the bright blue of* Ceratostigma plumbaginoides *in foreground.*

[57]

Chrysanthemum morifolium   **Hardy Chrysanthemum, Mum**
                                    Daisy Family (Compositae)

If any degree of perfection whatever is desired, these are probably the least recommended of all plants for a low maintenance situation, and little space can be devoted to them here, other than to list the faults. Annual division is necessary because healthy growth and flowering diminish after the first year. Mums are gross feeders and require frequent top-dressings during the growing season. Most all, except the low cushion varieties, must be pinched back several times during the earlier part of the summer to encourage branching and heavy flowering. Some of the large-flowering types should have the secondary flower buds removed. Spraying or dusting every two weeks with a complete pesticide often will be necessary. Although some varieties are quite hardy in our area, most are not reliably so and require the protection of a light mulch, or are better over-wintered in a cold frame. If the homeowner with little time wishes a bright autumnal display, it would be far better to purchase a few mums in pots; almost every garden center, florist, or roadside stand features them in the fall.

Chrysanthemum coccineum   **Pyrethrum, Painted Daisy**
                                   Daisy Family (Compositae)

From the standpoint of low maintenance, the Painted Daisies are one group in the Chrysanthemum clan which can be recommended. *Pyrethrum* is the old generic name; they are commonly called Pyrethrum and are so listed in catalogs rather than under *Chrysanthemum.*

They are of particular value for their bright, Daisy-like single or double blossoms in vibrant shades of pink to red or white, in June and early July. Another asset is the bright green, finely-divided foliage.

Painted Daisies perform best in a fairly rich soil that is well supplied with humus. They squarely belong in the group whose hardiness is lessened when the soil is soggy during the winter months, but are perfectly hardy in Boston when good drainage is assured. Best in full sun, they will tolerate light shade during part of the day. They have no important pest or disease problems and will not require staking; division will be necessary after the fourth year. Planting or dividing is always done in spring and the protection of a winter mulch is advisable the first winter following. Height ranges from about 9 inches to 2½ feet so Pyrethrums are suited either to the front or middle of the border. They are effective singly, but better in groups of three planted about a foot apart.

Of the over 20 cultivars currently available, the following is but a selection to demonstrate the color range. Plants do not take kindly to long periods in the mail, so are better obtained from local sources where possible.

C. coccineum 'Buckeye' — Deep rose-red, flecked white, semi-double. 2 feet.
Sources: 24; I

C. coccineum 'Crimson Giant' — Bright red, 4-inch, single flowers. 3½ feet.
Sources: 13,24,32; C,I

C. coccineum 'Eileen May Robinson' — Salmon-pink, single. 2 feet.
Source: 66

C. coccineum 'Helen' — Soft light pink, double. 2½ feet.
Sources: 20,24,32,66; I,J

C. coccineum 'Robinson's Crimson' — Crimson, single. 2 feet.
Sources: 24,67,69; B,I,J,L

C. coccineum 'Snowball' — Double white. 2½ feet.
Sources: 20,66; J

Chrysanthemum maximum   Shasta Daisy
                                          Daisy Family (Compositae)
    The requirement of division to maintain vigor every second or third year, and their somewhat unreliable hardiness in our area causes us, grudgingly, to place these in the "not recommended for low maintenance" category.
    The mostly white, single or double Daisy-like flowers are excellent for cutting and appear from June until frost on plants 2 to 4 high. Shasta Daisies prefer rich soil which is moist but well drained in the summer, and not soggy in winter. Most cultivars will be hardy in this area if this condition can be met. The single cultivars are best in full sun, but the doubles will be disappointing unless they receive partial shade. They are effective singly or in groups of three or more planted about a foot apart. Plants in seemingly good health may sometimes wilt and die for no apparent reason, especially in a wet summer. This demise is caused by Verticillium Rot, a fungus disease which attacks the roots. Sick plants should be discarded immediately.
    Shasta Daisies are almost a necessity in the cutting garden, so, despite the problems, flower arrangers will probably wish to

try a few. This list is but a selection of the nearly 40 cultivars currently available:

C. maximum **'Aglaya'** — Lace Shasta — Double white, petals very fringed. Robust and considered one of the hardiest. 2 feet.
Sources: 13,15,24,28,32,44,58,67; C,I,J,K,L

C. maximum **'Alaska'** — One of the most popular; perhaps the hardiest. Single, white with a yellow center; typical Daisy flower. Cut the plants back after the first flowering has finished in mid-July and they will bloom again. 2 feet.
Sources: 3,23,24,25,37,46,53,58,67,69; A,B,E,F,I,K,L

C. maximum **'Cobham Gold'** — Flowers cream-colored, with a gold flush. Large, double, with a high crest in the center. 2 feet.
Sources: 24,32; I,L

C. maximum **'Diener's Double'** — Double white with frilled petals. 2 feet.
Sources: 37; B,E,

C. maximum **'Esther Read'** — Double white. 18 inches.
Sources: 13,15,32,59; C,E,

C. maximum **'Horace Read'** — A sport of *C.* 'Esther Read' but not as free-flowering — Larger double white flowers about 4 inches across.
Sources: 13,15,29; C

C. maximum **'Little Miss Muffet'** — Quite dwarf, 14 inches high. Semidouble, white.
Sources: 3,13,24,32,49,58,66,69; C,I,J

C. maximum **'Majestic'** — Single, very large (4 to 5 inches); white with a small yellow center.
Sources: 13,15,24,44,67; C,I,K

C. maximum **'Marconi'** — Double white, up to 6-inch flowers with very frilled petals, long period of bloom. 2 feet.
Sources: 3,15,37,69; A,B,F,K,L

C. maximum **'Thomas Killin'** — Double white with cream-colored crested center. 18 inches.
Sources: 13,24,67; C,I,J,K

Cimicifuga   Snakeroot, Bugbane, Cohosh
                              Buttercup Family (Ranunculaceae)
These are stately plants 3 to 8 feet tall which, when well established, can be left alone almost indefinitely. The small white flowers are produced on long racemes well above the shiny compound leaves. Best used as single specimens at the middle or rear of the herbaceous border, Snakeroots adapt themselves

Cimicifuga racemosa — *Bugbane or Cohosh. The spire-like effect is most welcome in the perennial garden in midsummer.*

equally well to massing at the edge of a pond or stream, or even amongst shrubbery.

For best growth, a moist soil with a high organic content is necessary. If this condition can be provided, the plants may be grown in full sun; however, they are used more commonly in semishaded areas as they perform best in a cooler location. They will tolerate deep shade, but at the expense of best results.

C. dahurica — Dahurian Bugbane — Much-branched, it grows to a height of 4 to 5 feet. The creamy-white flowers appear in August and last into the fall.
Sources: 13; C

C. foetida (listed in some catalogs as *C. simplex*) — Kamchatka Bugbane — Much smaller, to 3 feet, and more branched from the base, with numerous spirelike spikes of flowers.
Sources: 13,66,68,69; C

C. 'Armleuchter' — A more vigorous selection of the preceding with somewhat larger flowers.
Source: 68

C. racemosa — Black Snakeroot, Cohosh, Bugbane — A native American, the most commonly grown species, and the tallest (5 to 8 feet depending on soil and location). Blooms in late June and the display is prolonged to early August by smaller lateral spikes of flowers from the main stem.
Sources: 13,14,26,27,46,66,67,68,69; B,C,

C. 'White Pearl' — Very compact, 3 to 4 feet tall. Pure white flowers.
Sources: 59,66,68

Clematis   Clematis
                    Buttercup Family (Ranunculaceae)
The numerous climbing woody varieties of *Clematis* are demanding when it comes to the proper conditions for good growth. The herbaceous kinds are somewhat less so, but few amateur gardeners know of their value. Although not as showy as the climbers, they bloom over a long period in the summer and, once established, become permanent additions to the garden. All provide flowers which are excellent for cutting, and when flowering is finished develop attractive, fluffy seed heads.

They require rich, well-drained soil and benefit from occasional applications of lime. Full sun or partial shade is satisfactory. They grow fairly large (3 to 4 feet tall) and a spacing of about 2 feet is necessary. Since they are slow to establish, gaps between plants may be filled with annuals for a few years. Like the climbers, herbaceous Clematis prefer cool soil conditions so a 2-inch covering of mulch is advisable in summer. They resent frequent cultivation around the roots; in fact, all lower parts of the plants are easily damaged.

C. heracleafolia* var. *davidiana — Blue Tube Clematis — The last of the herbaceous group to bloom, this bears tubular deep blue flowers in August and September. They are fragrant and produced in terminal and axillary clusters on 2½ to 3-foot-high stems which may require support. The foliage has a somewhat coarse appearance so it would be undesirable to feature this plant in the most prominent part of the border. Nevertheless, it is of value for the display of blue flowers so late in the season.
Sources: 24,59,66,67; I

***C. heracleafolia* var. *davidiana* 'Wyvale'** — A selection of the preceding with deeper blue flowers.
Sources: 24; I

***C. integrifolia* 'Coerulea'** — Solitary Clematis — Has 1½ inch porcelain-blue bell-shaped flowers. Although it attains a height of only 2 feet, the stems have a tendency to flop if not supported. Where staking is not done, allow plenty of room so that the plant will not crowd its neighbors. When given a moderately moist situation, or if watered during dry spells, it will bloom from June to August.
Sources: 13,32,67; C

C. recta — Ground Clematis — Less handsome than its selections, and less frequently grown. Taller than the preceding two species (3 to 4 feet) and best near the rear of the border. Freely produces terminal and axillary clusters of ¾-inch fragrant, tubular white flowers in June and July. The species and the following cultivars or varieties require staking to prevent the plants from flopping at flowering time.
Sources: 24; I

***C. recta* 'Grandiflora'** — Bears a profusion of white flowers in June and July. 3 feet.
Sources: 66,69

C. recta* var. *mandshurica — The most commonly grown form of this species, it is valuable for its fragrant, tubular white flowers in June and July. Quite vigorous in growth so allow about 3 feet for it to spread.
Sources: 59,67

***C. recta* 'Purpurea'** — A selection with purplish-green foliage. Flowers white.
Sources: 24; I

Convallaria majalis	**Lily-of-the-Valley**
	Lily Family (Liliaceae)

Little need be said of this plant by way of description. It is popular because it is so undemanding and versatile. The ability to colonize restricts its use in the perennial garden where it may become a nuisance by usurping space. Where there is room for it to romp, few plants are hardier and more adaptable. Permanent, tolerant of most soil conditions except the extremes, it is suited to sun or shade, but does better with some shade. It should be kept in mind that Lily-of-the-Valley is poisonous in all parts, and that young children are attracted to the orange-red berries appearing in late summer and fall. These fruits should be removed. The common white-flowered form is easily available.
Sources: 3,13,14,20,24,27,32,37,43,44,57,58,59,66,67,68,69; A, B,C,I,J,K,L

***C. majalis* 'Flora Plena'** — Quite rare, double white form.
Sources: 32,66

***C. majalis* 'Rosea'** — Very pale pink.
Sources: 1,13,30,32,58,59,66; C

***C. majalis* 'Striata'** — The leaves have creamy-white stripes.
Sources: 32,66

Coreopsis	**Coreopsis, Tickseed**
	Daisy Family (Compositae)

A few members of this large genus are excellent for the low maintenance border; but some lack complete hardiness, behave as biennials, or are best seen naturalized in a wild garden. They all are sun lovers and prefer a light, sandy, well-drained soil.

Coreopsis verticillata — *Thread-leaf Coreopsis*

With the exception of *C. lanceolata*, division probably will be necessary after the fourth year.

Yellow Daisy-like flowers over long periods in the summer, and finely textured foliage are their best attributes.

C. auriculata 'Nana' — Dwarf Eared Coreopsis — A small spreading plant 4 to 6 inches tall, bearing numerous small bright orange-yellow flowers from June to August. Suited to the front of the perennial garden. Plant in a group of three spaced about 10 inches apart.
Sources: 3,66

C. lanceolata — Perennial Coreopsis — This and its cultivar following are the best for the low maintenance garden. It thrives for years in a sunny spot without needing to be divided. The bright yellow Daisy-like flowers are about 2 inches across, on stems 2 feet high. Blooms for most of the summer.
Sources: 27; B

C. lanceolata 'Sunburst' — An excellent cultivar of the above with large, bright, semidouble yellow flowers.
Sources: 24,60,66,67,68,69; E,F,I,J,K,L

C. verticillata — Thread-leaf Coreopsis — This often is found in catalogs under the name "Golden Shower." It makes large dense clumps about 2 feet tall, and 2 to 3 feet wide, and although the individual bright yellow flowers are small, they are freely produced throughout most of the summer among the finely textured leaves. Another good feature of this plant is its ability to withstand dry soil conditions.
Sources: 3,13,24,66,68; B,C,I,J,K,L

C. 'Baby Sun' — A hybrid, usually raised from seed but fairly uniform in its bright yellow flowers. 20 inches tall and compact in growth.
Sources: 3,13,69; A,C,J,L

C. 'Mayfield Giant' — Another hybrid which grows 3 feet tall with 3-inch bright yellow flowers in June and July.
Sources: 3; K

Delphinium   **Delphinium, Larkspur**
Buttercup Family (Ranunculaceae)
 Few plants can approach the Pacific Hybrid Delphiniums for their bold effect in the border. However, the whole Delphinium clan is finicky in nature and cannot be guaranteed as long-lived in our area even with ideal conditions of site and care.
 The soil must be rich, well drained, and slightly alkaline. A position in full sun is preferred. Shady conditions lead to troubles with mildew, but plants can be affected by this in a sunny spot, too. Annual applications of a 5–10–10 fertilizer and a side-dressing during the growing season are necessary to produce vigorous growth. Staking the flower stems individually to prevent toppling is a must with the taller varieties. Plants should be cut back after the main period of bloom to induce a second flowering at the end of the season. Spraying with a fungicide and miticide at 10-day intervals during the growing season is frequently necessary to control mildew and cyclamen mites. The latter carry a blight disease which distorts the leaves and buds and causes them to turn black. Elaborate winter protection may be necessary. Sand or ashes placed around the crowns helps to prevent attack by slugs. After the ground has frozen, plants should be covered by a thick layer of hay or straw (2 to 3 inches). It often is safer to overwinter the plants in a cold frame.
 In the few situations where Delphiniums prosper, they will live for many years and require division when the clumps have become large. This usually is after the third or fourth year. However, as a rule they are best treated as short-lived perennials, or biennials.

D. elatum — Common Delphinium, Candle or Bee Larkspur — These are the large-flowered types so prized for their 4 to 6-foot columns of densely packed blooms. Individual flowers may be 2 inches or more across. They come in many colors and may be single, semidouble or double; self-colored, or bicolor. Many have a central "eye," often called a "bee," usually of a contrasting shade or color. The parentage of the modern garden types is not well known but *D. elatum* is certainly the principal species involved.

In this country the *D. elatum* types commonly offered are the Pacific Hybrids. These are as good as, if not better than, any of the strains developed by the English breeders. (Those of English origin include the 'Blackmore and Langdon Hybrids,' available from: 69, 70; J, and the 'Wrexham Hybrids,' available from: 37; K.) All the cultivars which follow belong to the Pacific Hybrid group. Many nurseries offer them as plants grown from seed, and although they do reproduce relatively true, some variation from the descriptions offered here may be expected.

D. elatum **'Pacific Hybrids'** — The following sources offer unnamed plants in a mixture of colors.
Sources: 16, 23, 28, 32, 68; J,K,L

D. **'Astolat'** — Shades of lavender and pink, with a black or gold "bee" at the center.
Sources: 15,20,44,58,59,60,66,69; A,B,E,L

D. **'Black Night'** — Shades of deep purple with a black "bee."
Sources: 20,37,46,58,59,60,66,69; A,B,E,F,K,L

D. **'Blue Bird'** — Shades of medium blue with a white "bee."
Sources: 15,25,44,66,69; A,B,E,K

D. **'Blue Jay'** — Shades of dark blue.
Sources: 15,59; E,K

D. **'Elaine'** — Shades of pink to rosy-lilac with a white "bee."
Sources: 3,13,32; C,E,K

D. **'Galahad'** — Pure white, no contrasting "bee."
Sources: 3,15,20,25,37,44,46,58,59,60,67,69; A,B,E,F,K,L

D. **'Guinevere'** — Outer petals light blue, inner petals lavender, white "bee."
Sources: 20,25,37,58,59,69; A,E,F,K,L

D. **'King Arthur'** — Deep violet with a white "bee."
Sources: 3,15,25,44,46,59,60,66,67,69; A,B,E,K,L

D. **'Percival'** — Pure white with a black "bee."
Sources: 59,66,69; E

D. **'Summer Skies'** — Soft blue with a white "bee."
Sources: 3,15,20,37,44,46,58,59,60,66,67,69; A,B,E,F,K,L

D. × *belladonna* — Garland Larkspur (Sometimes listed in garden books as *D. cheilanthum* var. *formosum*, but this is a garden race of mostly unknown parentage.) Garland Larkspurs differ from the hybrids in the *D. elatum* group in their open branching habit. They have numerous short spikes with a looser arrangement of flowers, and blossom for a longer period. They are quite susceptible to mildew problems and must be in a position where air circulation is good. Light blue flowers. Plants reach a height of 3 to 4 feet.
Sources: 3,13,59,69,70; B,C,J,K,L

D. × *belladonna* 'Bellamosa' — Dark blue-flowered form.
Sources: 3,67,68,69; B,J,K,L

D. × *belladonna* 'Casa Blanca' — Pure white-flowered form. A vigorous grower which attains a height of nearly 5 feet.
Sources: 13,24,25,29,67,68,69; C,I,K,L

D. × *belladonna* 'Cliveden Beauty' — Sky blue flowers. Plants 3 feet in height.
Sources: 24,28,67; I,L

D. × *belladonna* 'Lamartine' — Flowers deep purplish-blue. Plants 3 feet in height.
Sources: 13,28; B,C,

D. 'Connecticut Yankee' — A comparatively new race of hybrids which are exceptionally free flowering and form densely branched plants 2½ feet in height. The 2 to 2½-inch blossoms are loosely arranged on the spikes and have a color range including shades of blue, purple, lavender, and white.
Sources: 13,14,20,24,25,28,68,69; A,B,C,E,I,J,K,L

D. *grandiflorum* — (The species and its forms invariably are listed in catalogs as *D. chinense*) — Siberian or Bouquet Larkspur — Members of this group are best treated as biennials in our area. They bloom in late summer, have a slender branching habit, and grow to 1½ to 2 feet in height. The flowers are violet-blue or white.
Sources: 24,46; I

D. *grandiflorum* 'Album' — White flowers.
Sources: 24,69; I

D. *grandiflorum* 'Blue Mirror' — Gentian-blue flowers.
Source: 69

D. *grandiflorum* 'Cambridge Blue' — Rich light blue flowers.
Source: 69

Dianthus   Pink, Carnation
Carnation Family (Caryophyllaceae)
This is a genus which contains many garden varieties. Considered in relation to their stature, they fall into two fairly distinct groups. The shorter, mat-forming types require conditions

Dicentra spectabilis — *Bleeding Heart*

of excellent soil drainage and are best in the rock garden. Many of these thrive in the Boston area. The taller types are suitable for the perennial border, but are distressingly short-lived, or extremely intolerant of the hot, humid weather frequently experienced during the summer in our area.

Dicentra   **Bleeding Heart, Lyre Flower**
Fumitory Family (Fumariaceae)

For permanence, the best of this group is *D. spectabilis*, the Bleeding Heart or Lyre Flower. It is a true aristocrat of the border for the short period when it is in bloom. A well-established plant forms a large clump 2½ feet tall and up to 2½ to 3 feet broad with arching stems bearing pink heart-shaped flowers in late May and June. It prefers a rich soil well supplied with organic matter and results are always best if light shade can be provided. Specimen plants are preferable to groupings because each requires a lot of room. If they are situated in full sun, the

foliage has a tendency to die down in the hot part of the summer, leaving a large gap in the border. For this reason Bleeding Hearts are frequently planted near *Gypsophila paniculata* (Baby's Breath). By the time the former is about to disappear, *Gypsophila* is ready to mask the gaps. Other plants which will act as fillers include *Hosta, Hemerocallis*, or even annuals. *Dicentra spectabilis* is a very long-lived plant which dislikes being disturbed. It is best planted only in the spring before new growth commences, and in a place where it can be left alone for many years.

Sources: 3,7,13,14,23,24,28,30,32,37,39,46,58,59,67,68,69; B,C, G,H,I,J,K,L

D. eximia — Plume or Fringed Bleeding Heart — This species is of great value for its long flowering period from May to August. The dissected leaves are grayish-blue, remain attractive throughout the growing season, and make a good contrast to the pink flowers. The flowers are a paler pink and smaller than *D. spectabilis*, but have the same overall heart-shaped form. *D. eximia* will not die back if planted in full sun, yet is perfectly adaptable to conditions of light shade. It grows from 12 to 18 inches tall, and is best seen in groups of three or more planted about a foot apart near the front of the garden. Plants may require division after the fourth year, but are best left alone until the clumps begin to deteriorate.

Sources: 1,3,7,13,24,28,37,39,46,57,58,66,68; B,C,H,I,J,K,L

Flowers of Dicentra eximia

Several cultivars are presently available which, in general, resemble *D. eximia* in habit of growth and have the same general cultural requirements. Their flowers range in color from pink to deep pink, or almost red, and some have a flowering period considerably longer than *D. eximia*. Confusion exists as to the exact parentage of some of these forms and they frequently are listed under the name *D. eximia*, but are hybrids involving *D. eximia*, *D. formosa* (Western Bleeding Heart), or *D. oregona*. They all grow to a height of about a foot. Those advertised to bloom intermittently through the summer should have faded blossoms removed at frequent intervals for best results.

D. 'Adrian Bloom' — Crimson-red flowers. Blue-green foliage. Forms large clumps, about a foot tall.
Sources: 13,24,29; C,I

D. 'Bountiful' — Deep pink flowers. Blue-green foliage. Produces intermittent blossoms in the summer after the main flowering period in May. Has another period of heavy flowering in early autumn.
Sources: 59,66,67

D. 'Luxuriant' — Flower buds cherry-red, flowers red. Green foliage. Blossoms intermittently until frost.
Sources: 57; K

Dicentra eximia — *Fringed Bleeding Heart*

[71]

D. 'Summer Beauty' — Deep rose flowers. Gray-green foliage. Blossoms into the summer.
Sources: 24,32; I

D. 'Valentine' — A new introduction, flowers described by the introducer as Spiraea-red. Recurrent blossoms until frost following the main blooming period in late April or May.
Source: 67

D. 'Zestful' — Deep rose flowers. Gray-green foliage. Blossoms through the summer.
Sources: 7,14,20; L

Dictamnus albus **Gas Plant, Dittany, Burning Bush Citrus Family (Rutaceae)**

Dictamnus albus (usually listed in catalogs as *D. fraxinella*), is one of the most permanent perennials in the garden. The best treatment is simply to leave the plants alone, and they will increase in vigor as each year passes. In fact, the best way to ruin a good clump of *Dictamnus* is to divide it and attempt to re-establish the resulting plants elsewhere. For this reason, it is advisable to begin with young plants of seedling size, preferably started in pots. Even then it may take several seasons before they give the desired effect, but the results will be worth waiting for.

Although it will tolerate partial shade, a sunny location with moderately rich soil is best for the Gas Plant. Situations which remain wet for any length of time should be avoided, and the plant can be counted upon to withstand moderate periods of drought. Although it is slow to start, a well-grown specimen will take up a lot of room in the border and it is best to leave about 2 to 2½ feet in each direction for expansion. Annuals could be used to fill the gaps in the meantime. A well-grown Gas Plant will eventually attain a height of 3 feet, and is of value as a specimen plant in the background of the small garden, or as a middle-of-the-border subject, especially when combined with shrubs. Staking will never be necessary. The 2-inch flowers are grouped in terminal racemes and appear for about two weeks during June. The relatively short period of blossom has been listed as a disadvantage, but the handsome, pinnate leaves remain in good condition throughout the season and provide an excellent accent wherever the plant is placed. When crushed, bruised, or

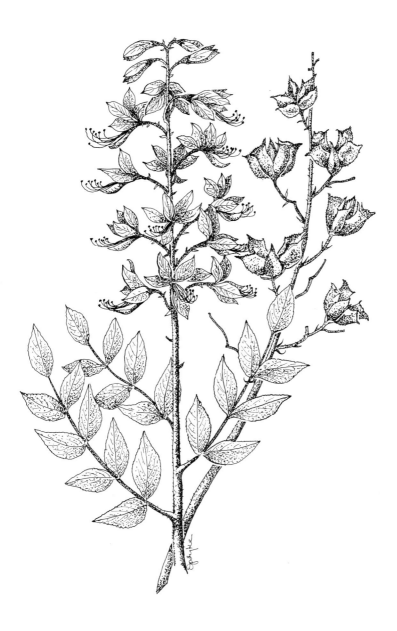

Dictamnus albus — *Gas Plant*

even brushed against, leaves and stems emit a pleasant fragrance of lemons. The fruits remain on the plant well into the winter and provide interest long after the flowers have gone. They are very useful in dried arrangements.

The name Gas Plant or Burning Bush is derived from the fact that the plant exudes a volatile gas just below the flowers, and this can be ignited by a match without harm to the plant. A small blue flame of very short duration is produced, but conditions must be quite calm as the gas is easily dispersed by breezes. It is often stated that the best conditions for producing this phenomenon exist on calm sultry evenings when the plants are in full flower.

D. albus — Flowers pure white.
Sources: 3,4,13,24,32,46,59,67,69; C,I

D. albus var. purpureus (usually listed in catalogs as var. *ruber*) — Deep pink or purplish flowers with deeper colored veins.
Sources: 3,13,14,24,25,32,59,67,68,69; C,I

Digitalis   Foxglove
Figwort Family (Scrophulariaceae)
Well-loved for their spirelike stalks with pink, white, yellow, or rosy purple flowers in midsummer, most Foxgloves are biennials. They will often perpetuate themselves by self-sowing, but cannot be relied upon to do so in all situations. There are a few perennial species which are of quite easy culture, but they are not particularly showy and space should not be wasted upon them, especially in a small garden.

All Foxgloves prefer a location in light shade and a fairly fertile soil which does not dry out quickly during the summer. Soggy soil conditions in winter are usually fatal. Plants should be discarded as soon as the seeds are dispersed, as the dying foliage becomes unsightly by August.

D. grandiflora — Yellow Foxglove — Frequently listed in nursery catalogs by the old name, *D. ambigua*. It grows to a height of 3 feet and, although advertised frequently as a true perennial, is best treated as a biennial. The 2-inch pale yellow flowers have brown blotches in the throats, appear in July, and are not particularly striking.
Sources: 13,24,25,29,32,69; C,I,K

D. 'Mertonensis' — Showiest and most nearly perennial of all the types commonly available. One of the best for a low maintenance garden. The Strawberry-red flowers appear on 3 to 3½-foot stems in June and July.
Sources: 13,14,24,29,32,66,69; C,I

Digitalis purpurea 'Excelsior Hybrid'

***D. purpurea* 'Excelsior Hybrids'** — Most effective of the *D. pur-purea* group because the flowers are borne all around the spike, rather than on one side. They come in many beautiful pastel shades of pink, mauve, yellow, and white with attractive deep mottling in the throat of each. They attain heights of 4 to 5 feet. The spirelike habit is most welcome in the garden during the month of June.
Sources: 13,24,68,69; A,B,C,E,J,K,L

***D. purpurea* 'Shirley Hybrids'** — The progenitors of the 'Excelsior Hybrids,' these come in the same array of colors, but the flowers are borne on one side of the spike only.
Sources: 13,23,24; C,E,I,K,L

***D. purpurea* 'Hyacinth Hybrids'** — Similar to the 'Shirley Hybrids' with a color range including white, shell-pink, and deep rose. Throats of the flowers are mottled with crimson or chocolate.
Source: 67

D. thapsi — Although native to Spain, this species is quite hardy and has good perennial tendencies. It is fairly similar in appearance to the wild forms of *D. purpurea*. The flowers are basically cream-colored, suffused with Strawberry-pink. Plants grow to a height of 2½ to 3 feet.
Source: 29

Doronicum   Doronicum, Leopardsbane
                                Daisy Family (Compositae)

These plants are valued for their 2 to 3-inch bright yellow, Daisy-like flowers in May. Apart from the display they make in the garden, the flowers are excellent for cutting purposes.

Doronicums will tolerate a position either in full sun or partial shade, but the soil should be well supplied with humus for the root systems are quite shallow. The leaves begin to deteriorate, or disappear entirely, in midsummer so it is wise not to make large groupings. Although reputed to require division every two years, the plants may remain undisturbed for four years or more. Division, when indicated, usually is done in August or very early spring before new growth commences. Depending upon variety, Doronicums may be planted either at the front or middle of the border. Allow them to be close enough to plants with spreading foliage so that gaps will be filled in when the Doronicums disappear in summer.

D. caucasicum — Caucasian Leopardbane — Flowers about 2 inches across, borne one to a stem. Stems about 12 to 15 inches

high when in flower. Leaves kidney-shaped, serrated at the edges. Plants of low, creeping habit.
Sources: 3,14,66,67,68; A,K

D. caucasicum var. magnificum — Flowers 2½ inches. Otherwise about the same as the preceding.
Sources: 24,39,66,69; I,J,L

D. caucasicum 'Madam Mason' — Similar to D. *caucasicum* var. *magnificum* in flower, but the foliage tends to be somewhat more persistent in summer than that of the species.
Sources: 13,32,59,66,67,68; C

D. plantagineum — Showy Leopardsbane — Flowers up to 3 inches across on plants 3 to 5 feet. Very showy in flower, but considered coarse in overall appearance compared to the others.
Source: 66

Several other species and cultivars of *Doronicum* are frequently described in books on perennials. None of them appears readily available from nurseries at the present time.

Echinacea purpurea   **Purple or Hedgehog Coneflower**
                                         Daisy Family (Compositae)
In general appearance this plant is very stiff and coarse and is best seen naturalized well away from the perennial garden or more formal plantings. It will vary in height from 3 to 5 feet and has large bristly leaves and purplish flowers with ray petals which droop in a rather unattractive manner.

There are several named varieties which invariably are listed as cultivars of E. *purpurea*. Undoubtedly they are hybrids derived from crossing E. *purpurea* with several other species; they frequently are found in catalogs under *Rudbeckia*. All are much more refined in appearance, bloom over long periods in dry soil, and reach heights of 3 to 4 feet. They are best in well-drained, sandy soils in either full sun or light shade. The stems are very sturdy and staking is not required. Division after the fourth year often will be necessary. About their only real drawback is that the flowers are prone to attack by Japanese beetles; therefore Purple Coneflowers probably should not be grown extensively where these insects are a problem and spraying cannot be done regularly.
Sources: 4,27,29,39,59,60; A,B,K,L

Echinacea purpurea — *Purple Coneflower*

E. ✕ **'Bright Star'** — Bright rose-red, 2½ to 3-inch, Daisy-like flowers with maroon-red centers; plants 2½ to 3 feet.
Sources: 24,67; I

E. ✕ **'Robert Bloom'** — Vigorous, freely branching plant, with 2½ to 3-inch carmine-purple flowers with orange centers. 2½ to 3 feet.
Sources: 66,67

Echinops ritro — *Steel Globe Thistle*

E. × 'The King' — 3-inch coral-crimson flowers with maroon or brownish centers. 3 feet.
Sources: 13,24,32,66,67,68; C,I

E. × 'White Lustre' — The only cultivar offered with white flowers. Blossoms heavily, even in times of drought, but the leaves are quite coarse and the petals are inclined to droop in an ungainly manner.
Sources: 13,24,32,66,67; C,I

Echinops   **Globe Thistle**
                                Daisy Family (Compositae)
   If one is unfamiliar with the appearance of Globe Thistles, it would be prudent to observe them growing in a garden setting before deciding whether or not to obtain some plants. Some people object to the rather coarse general appearance and the harshness of the Thistle-like leaves. Others, including those who like to arrange cut flowers, prize the blue globular flowerheads which are made up of many spiny bracts and flowers. These appear in midsummer to early fall, are excellent for cutting, and may be dried easily for winter arrangements. The leaves are white on the undersurface and give character to the plant. Whatever one's opinion, these are bold plants which seldom fail to attract comment.

Although Globe Thistles will tolerate partial shade, a position in full sun gives best results. The soil should be well drained and need not be unusually fertile. Plants will endure considerable exposure to dry conditions, but prefer soil of average moisture retention; wet, soggy conditions should be avoided, however.

Plants form dense clumps which never require staking. They are best seen arranged in a fairly bold group of about three at the middle or rear of the border. Division is not necessary for many years, but is an arduous chore because established clumps have very extensive root systems about a foot deep. New plants will sprout up from old roots left in the ground so replanting is seldom necessary.

E. 'Taplow Blue' — The best cultivar. Rich steel-blue flower heads with a silvery overcast, up to 3 inches in diameter. Plants bushy, 4 to 5 feet tall. Blooms in August.
Sources: 3,13,21,24,32,67,69; C,I,L

E. ritro — Steel Globe Thistle — Blue flowers, somewhat variable in color, on 3 to 5-foot plants.
Sources: 39,45,46,66,68; A,B,E,J,L

E. sphaerocephalus — Common Globe Thistle — Flowers silvery-gray; plants 5 to 6 feet tall.
Source: 45

Epimedium   Barrenwort, Bishop's Hat
                               Barberry Family (Berberidaceae)

This group is well known to a number of advanced gardeners, but has been neglected undeservedly by the majority of the gardening public in this country. Barrenworts' greatest value is as foliage plants. The delicate pinnate leaves are semi-evergreen in winter; new leaves in spring are pale green tinted with a delicate shade of rose, and often have pink veins. In summer they become a deep glossy green, mottled with purple in some varieties. The cooler weather of autumn brings out an attractive crimson coloration.

The old foliage should be cut back to the ground in late winter or very early spring to enhance the beauty of newly unfolding leaves and to show off the flowers. Although these are small (about ½-inch) they are as handsome as some orchids. They are cup-shaped with conspicuous long spurs, and are borne

Epimedium grandiflorum

on numerous stems 8 to 12 inches high. According to variety, colors may range from red to yellow, white, rose or lilac.

Barrenworts are most accommodating in their ease of culture. Although most frequently grown in light shade, they will thrive at the front of the border in full sun if the soil is fairly moist during the summer months. In a shady position they will tolerate considerably drier conditions, but very dry places should be avoided. One of the great unsung virtues of the plants is their ability to grow at the base of a tree, a situation which few other perennials will tolerate due to root competition. Many perennial gardens are planned around small trees such as crab apples or magnolias, and underplanting often poses a problem. *Epimedium* is frequently the best plant to use, treated as a ground cover.

These are very long-lived plants and division will usually be necessary only for purposes of propagation. This is best done in early spring or early fall. Barrenworts are best seen planted in small groupings of at least three, spaced about 10 inches apart. The plants spread in a modest way, but never to the point of becoming invasive, so it would be wise to allow at least a foot of space around them to accommodate this tendency and prevent crowding by taller neighboring plants.

Unfortunately, in the case of this group, incorrect names abound in the nursery trade. Although many others are described in text books, the following appear to be all that are offered at the present time by dealers in perennials. A few not listed here might be found in the catalogs of nurseries specializing in rock garden and alpine plants.

E. grandiflorum var. *album* — Flowers white. Plants about 10 to 12 inches tall.
Source: 66

E. grandiflorum 'Rose Queen' — Flowers bright rose, spurs tipped with white.
Sources: 29,66

E. pinnatum — Flowers bright yellow with very short brownish-purple spurs. Plants 8 to 12 inches tall. Plants obtained from nurseries under this name are often the variety *colchicum* which has fewer leaflets than the species.
Sources: 66,67

E. pinnatum 'Snow Queen' — Flowers white. Plants 10 inches tall.
Source: 66

E. × *rubrum* (*E. alpinum* × *E. grandiflorum*) — Large 1-inch bright crimson flowers, flushed yellow or white. The showiest variety in flower. New leaves red in spring. Sometimes listed under the name *E. alpinus* var. *roseum.*
Sources: 13,32,67,68; C

E. × *versicolor* 'Sulphureum' (*E. grandiflorum* × *E. pinnatum* var. *colchicum*), sometimes listed as *E. pinnatum* var. *sulphureum* or *E. sulphureum* — Flowers yellow. Leaves have a pinkish tinge in autumn.
Sources: 13,32,49,66,67,68,69; C

E. × *warleyense* (probably *E. alpinum* × *pinnatum* var. *colchicum*) — Sepals coppery-red, petals yellow, spurs yellow streaked with red. Plants about 12 inches high and quite vigorous of growth.
Source: 68

Erigeron 'Pink Jewel'

E. × ***youngianum* 'Niveum'** (probably *E. diphyllum* × *E. grandiflorum*) — Sometimes listed as *E. macranthum* var. *niveum*. Flowers white. Plants about 9 to 10 inches and of compact habit.
Sources: 13,49,66,67,68,69; C

E. × ***youngianum* 'Roseum'** (sometimes listed as *E. macranthum* var. *lilacinum* or *E. lilacinum*) — Flowers clear purplish-mauve.
Sources: 49,66,67, 68

***E.* 'White Flower Hybrid #1'** — Flowers red and yellow.
Source: 69

Erigeron   Fleabane
Daisy Family (Compositae)

Although quite similar in flower to the Fall Asters, this group blooms earlier (June and early July) and does not need frequent division if the soil is light and sandy with good drainage. Diversity of color and height are far more restricted than with the Asters, but most varieties can be left in place for four years before clumps begin to deteriorate.

They demand a position in full sun. Flowers are excellent for cutting; it is said that frequent removal of old blossoms will help to prolong the blooming season.

Fleabanes are more appreciated in Europe, particularly England, than they are here. The lower growing cultivars frequently have been used in rock gardens; when brought into the perennial border, they are best planted in groups of at least three to produce a strong effect. Fleabanes are good plants to try where soils are relatively dry and infertile, otherwise there are many showier plants which bloom at the same time.

E. aurantiacus — Orange Daisy or Fleabane — Semidouble, bright orange flowers up to 2 inches across in July and August on plants about 9 inches high. Perhaps the showiest of the group in flower, but may not be quite as hardy as some of the others.
Sources: 24; I

E. speciosus — Oregon Fleabane — Narrow, violet-blue petals, yellow centers. Plants 18 inches to 2 feet tall. Bloom in late June and July, then with sporadic flowers to September.
Sources: 69; J,K,L

E. 'Double Beauty' — Double violet-blue flowers with yellow centers. Plants 18 to 24 inches tall.
Sources: 13,24,32; C,I

E. 'Foerster's Liebling' (also listed as 'Foerster's Darling') — Flowers bright pink with yellow centers, semidouble. Plants 18 to 24 inches tall.
Sources: 13,24,49,67,69; C,I

E. 'Pink Jewel' — Flowers lavender-pink with yellow centers. Plants 18 to 24 inches tall.
Source: G

E. 'Prosperity' — Flowers mauve-blue, nearly double. Plants 18 inches tall.
Sources: 24,66; I

E. 'Red Beauty' — Flowers ruby-red with yellow centers. Plants 15 to 18 inches tall.
Sources: 28; K

> *E. compositus* — Fernleaf Fleabane — Flowers white. Plants 4 to 6 inches tall. Blooms in early sring. More suited to the rock garden.
> Source: 29

> *E. linearis* — Narrow-Leaved Fleabane — Flowers yellow. Plants 8 inches tall. More suited to the rock garden.
> Source: 29

Eryngium   Sea Holly, Eryngo
                            Carrot Family (Umbelliferae)
Deserving of more frequent cultivation, these are ideal plants for sunny areas where the soil is sandy and remains dry, especially in winter.

Eryngium planum

[84]

Sea Hollies are Thistle-like in appearance, usually are planted as a single specimen or in twos; they do not lend themselves to massing. Although they give a bold effect, it is not a coarse one. They are very long-lived. The species recommended here develop deep fleshy roots, and resent disturbance of any sort. They range from 1½ to 3 feet in height, the wiry stems do not require staking, and there are no insect or disease problems. The rather unorthodox flowers make interesting subjects for arrangements, and if picked when fully open, retain their color when dried.

E. alpinum — Bluetop Eryngo — Perhaps the most beautiful of the group, it is the only one that will tolerate light shade and somewhat heavier soil conditions. The 2-inch flower heads are a beautiful silvery-blue. The uppermost leaves or bracts just below the flower heads are pointed or jagged and have this color also. The lower leaves are deeply heart-shaped and toothed. Plants grow to a height of 18 to 20 inches; the flowers appear in August and last through September.
Source: 29

E. amethystinum — Amethyst Sea Holly — Lower growing, not over 1½ to 2 feet in height. The flowers, bracts, and upper stems are steel-gray shading to amethyst in color. The leaves are deeply cut and spiny. Blooms in July and August.
Sources: 13,24,66,67,69; C,I

E. bourgati — Mediterranean Sea Holly — Flowers and long bracts steel-blue. Plants about 1½ feet in height. Blooms from June to August.
Source: 29

E. planum — Rounded, small blue flower heads on stems which branch more than the other species, thus are denser in growth. Plants grow to 3 feet in height and may require staking unless the soil is poor.
Source: E

E. 'Violetta' — Large violet-blue flowers. Plants about 2 to 2½ feet in height.
Sources: 24; I

Eupatorium coelestinum   **Mist Flower, Hardy Ageratum**
                                      Daisy Family (Compositae)

Only one species in this genus is appropriate in the perennial border; all others are more suitable when naturalized in wild gardens or woodlands. *E. coelestinum* is native from New Jersey to Florida and Texas, and its blue or lavender flowers can be used in the same manner as Asters to provide a contrast to the yellow, orange, and bronze colors of many autumn flowering plants. It resembles *Ageratum* when in bloom and some people will mistake it for that plant even though it flowers in late summer and is taller, growing to a height of 2 feet.

The blossoms are excellent for cutting, and dry well if picked just before opening.

Mist Flower does best in full sun in an ordinary well-drained garden soil, and also will tolerate partially shaded conditions. Plants spread rapidly by underground stems and will require division after the second or third year to keep them in bounds and in good appearance. They appear late in the spring, so early cultivation should be done with care.

Sources: 24,39,59,66,69; B,G,I,K

E. coelestinum var. *album* — White-flowered form of the species.
Sources: 39; B

E. coelestinum 'Wayside Variety' — A somewhat more compact form of the species with pale lavender flowers. Plants are 12 to 14 inches in height.
Sources: 13,32,67; C

Euphorbia   **Spurge**
                              Spurge Family (Euphorbiaceae)

Several members of this large and varied family of both temperate and tropical areas are of outstanding value in a low maintenance situation. They require full sun and a porous, somewhat sandy soil of ordinary fertility; if encouraged by anything more than a "lean diet" they may spread rapidly and lose their value. The varieties recommended here all are long-lived and dislike being transplanted. They appear to be immune to insect or disease problems. Flowers are relatively long lasting and make excellent subjects for arrangements if the cut ends of the stem are charred by a match and plunged into deep water. As with their well-known relatives, the Poinsettias, the true flowers appear in small clusters surrounded by the more showy petal-like leaves called bracts.

E. corollata — Flowering Spurge — An American species which grows to a height of about 2 feet and produces numerous flower clusters with small white bracts in July and August. It is similar in appearance to *Gypsophila* (Baby's Breath), in blossom, and when cut the flowers have the same use. Gives a refined, lacy effect in the garden. The leaves turn red in the fall.
Sources: 24; I

E. epithymoides — Cushion Spurge — Almost always listed in nursery catalogs as *E. polychroma*, this is a neat, symmetrical, mound-like plant for the front of the border. It grows to a height of 1 to 1½ feet and produces globular umbels of bright chartreuse-yellow bracts from the end of April through May. The leaves turn red in the fall.
Sources: 13,14,24,32,57,59,66,67,68,69; A,C,I,K,L

E. myrsinites — Myrtle Euphorbia — Probably best as a rock garden plant, but of use at the front of a border if soil conditions are especially dry. This species produces stems about 1 to 1½ feet long which are never over a few inches high because they trail over the ground. The leaves are blue-green and remain on the plant through the winter. Flowers appear in clusters at the ends of the stems in late April and early May. The plant self-sows, but seldom freely enough to become a nuisance.
Sources: 32,66,67; L

Filipendula   **Filipendula, Meadow Sweet, Dropwort**
Rose Family (Rosaceae)

Filipendulas are grown for their feathery terminal clusters of numerous small flowers. Some may be large plants 4 to 6 feet high and suitable only for the back of the border or in combination with shrubs; or in woodland or streamside plantings. The taller types require moist soils with a fairly high humus content, and some shade. These all are long-lived plants which do not require frequent division.

F. hexapetala — Dropwort — Seldom exceeds 2 feet in height and is the only Filipendula suited to the front of the border. Tolerates full sun and dry soil conditions. The finely divided fernlike foliage is especially pleasing and can be used to advantage to tone down the appearance of coarser plants. Creamy-white flower panicles are produced in June.
Sources: 32,68

F. hexapetala 'Flore-plena' — Double Dropwort— A form with double white flowers. Smaller in stature, about 15 to 18 inches tall, and suited to the front of the border.
Sources: 4,32,66,67,68

F. purpurea 'Elegans' — cultivar of Japanese Meadow Sweet — (sometimes listed as *F. palmata* var. *elegans*) — Grows to a height of 2 to 4 feet depending upon soil conditions. Flowers white with bright red stamens.
Sources: 32,66

E. rubra — Queen-of-the-Prairie — One of the best back-of-the-border plants. Grows from 4 to 6 feet tall and produces large terminal clusters of small pink flowers in June and July.
Sources: 32,66

F. rubra var. venusta — Martha Washington Plume — Fragrant, deep pink flowers in 12-inch clusters in July and early August. Considered far superior to the species but presently difficult to obtain.
Source: 66

F. ulmaria — Queen-of-the-Meadow — Another tall species which will reach 4 feet in height under good conditions. Fragrant white flowers from mid-June to mid-July. This is a Eurasian species which is now rather widely naturalized in parts of New England. It does not seem to be available at the present time, but the following cultivars can be recommended.

F. ulmaria 'Aurea Variegata' — A rare form with leaves variegated with creamy-yellow.
Source: 32

F. ulmaria 'Flore-Plena' — Double-flowered form of the preceding.
Sources: 32,66

Gaillardia   **Blanket Flower**
                                    Daisy Family (Compositae)
     Gaillardias can cause great disappointment unless they are grown in a very well-drained soil. Many types sprawl unless staked early, and the best ones are seldom very hardy. Some people are greatly attached to the bright colors of the Daisy-like flowers; others think them too gaudy. Many varieties have an extended period of blossom throughout the summer, but because

of their tendency to be only temporary residents of the garden, they cannot be recommended here.

G. *aristata* — Common Perennial Gaillardia — The principal parent of the modern cultivars. Native in the western U.S.A. Flowers basically yellow, but may have purple to red blotches at the base of the petals.
Source: 46

G. 'Baby Cole' — Probably the best of all the cultivars, and perhaps more permanent than most. The dwarfest; plants 6 inches high. Large red flowers, tipped with yellow.
Sources: 24,29,60; I,K

G. 'Burgundy' — Large wine-red flowers up to 3 inches across. 30-inch plants.
Sources: 3,13,25,30,39,49,68,69; A,B,C,E,K,L

G. 'Dazzler' — Bright, golden-yellow flowers with maroon centers. Plants 2 to 3 feet tall.
Sources: 3,25,58,68; B,E,J,K,L

G. 'Goblin' — Flowers deep red with yellow tips on the petals. Plants 1 foot tall.
Sources: 3,13,49,68,69; A,B,C,E,K

G. 'Portola' — A strain raised from seed. Flowers in various combinations of red and yellow. Plants about 30 inches tall.
Sources: 69; K

G. 'Sun Dance' — Dwarf, compact plants about 8 inches in height. Red centers and petals which have yellow tips.
Source: 67

G. 'Yellow Queen' — Buff or chamois-yellow flowers. Plants 2 feet tall.
Sources: 67; L

Geranium   Cranesbill
Geranium Family (Geraniaceae)

Sometimes confused with *Pelargonium* (whose common name is Geranium), this is a showy group of great value for summer bedding and as pot plants. True geraniums come from temperate parts of the world. A number of the handsome species are hardy as far north as Boston and among them are several which adapt well to low maintenance plantings.

They are low mound-like plants, seldom over a foot high and best for positions at the front of the perennial garden. The lower growing varieties are highly adaptable to rock garden conditions. Blooming is best in full sun, but results are nearly as good in partial shade. Flowers vary in size from an inch to nearly 2 inches and are produced fairly freely throughout most of the summer. Rampant growth is encouraged by an overly fertile soil. All species discussed here can be left undivided for a minimum of four years, often longer. When the clumps begin to deteriorate, division is best performed in the spring.

G. cinereum 'Ballerina' — Lilac-colored flowers with dark red veins and center. Plants 4 inches high.
Sources: 24; I

G. cinereum 'Splendens' — Screeching magenta flowers 1 inch across with dark blotches at the base of each petal. Flowers

Gaillardia aristata *cultivar*

freely all summer. Plants 3 to 4 inches.
Source: 69

G. dalmaticum — Light pink flowers with deeper veins; produced freely in May and June. Plants 4 inches.
Sources: 13,24,32,39,49,58,66,67,69; C,I,J,L

G. dalmaticum var. album — White-flowered form of the preceding species, very pale pink at the center.
Sources: 13,66,69; C

G. endressii — Much taller in stature, 15 to 18 inches, and can be used further back in the border. Flowers light rose with somewhat darker veins. Cut back after the first flowering in May for more flowers late in the summer. The two cultivars which follow are better color forms than the species.
Sources: 32,49

G. endressii 'Johnson's Blue' — Good light blue. Flowers very heavily produced but may not last as long in bloom as the species. Plants 15 to 18 inches.
Sources: 67,68

G. endressii 'Wargrave Pink' — Flowers clear pink, produced over most of the summer. Plants 15 to 18 inches.
Sources: 13,67; C

G. grandiflorum — See G. meeboldii

G. ibericum — Iberian Cranesbill — Violet-blue flowers with darker veins. Blossoms during June and July. Plants 2 feet in height when in flower.
Source: 67

G. meeboldii — Lilac Cranesbill — The recent change of name is, perhaps, unfortunate for a plant so firmly entrenched in garden circles as G. grandiflorum, (as it is listed in all catalogs.) Large 1½ to 2-inch magenta flowers with reddish veins; blooms May into July. 18 to 24 inches in height when in flower. Individual plants form clumps about a foot wide.
Sources: 3,24,32,67,69; I

G. meeboldii var. alpinum — Flowers 1½ inches across and close to true blue. Plants about 12 inches high with deeply lobed foliage.
Sources: 13; C,K

Geranium sanguineum *var.* prostratum

G. meeboldii 'Plenum' — Double purple-blue flowers in May and June.
Sources: 13,49,66; C

G. sanguineum — Bloodred Geranium, Bloody Cranesbill — Forms large clumps 1½ to 2 feet in diameter. Fine in an ordinary situation, but excessive spreading is encouraged by overly rich soil conditions. Flowers purple-red from May to August. Deep red autumn foliage coloration. Plants about 12 inches high.
Sources: 4,32,66

G. sanguineum var. ***album*** — White-flowered form of the preceding species.
Sources: 3,32,68

G. sanguineum var. ***prostratum*** — Often listed in catalogs as *G. lancastriense* or *G. sanguineum* var. *lancastriense*. Much more compact in growth than the species and not as rampant. About 6 inches in height. Bright pink blossoms with reddish veins. Flowers most of the summer.
Sources: 1,3,13,24,32,59,66,68; C,I

Geum   Geum, Avens
                                              Rose Family (Rosaceae)

Geums have had a bad name among some gardeners in the Boston area. Many people have heard glowing reports of the wonderful flower colors but have been dismayed when their newly acquired plants died during the first winter.

G. coccineum, a species with bright orange-red flowers, is native to Asia Minor and Southern Europe. Breeders have selected hardy forms of this and crossed them with a somewhat less hardy species, *G. chiloense* (the Scarlet Avens from Chile), to produce a remarkably showy and valuable group of cultivars. These are relatively hardy in our area and do not require the biennial divisions necessary to maintain some of the older selections which are seldom available today. Despite this, Geums cannot be recommended for general use here, for not all gardeners will succeed with this group.

Geums prefer a spot in full sun and a well-drained soil which contains as much organic matter as possible for moisture retention in the summer. Soggy winter conditions are fatal. The plants are slow to increase in size, and may not produce a great show of either leaves or flowers until the second or third year. The cultivars discussed here will go for many years before division is necessary for purposes of rejuvenation.

Plants usually attain a height of 2½ to 3 feet. They are most effective in groups of three planted 12 to 18 inches apart. Geums bloom freely from about mid-May to August, and intermittently thereafter if seed formation is prevented by removing the faded flowers.

G. × borisii (*G. bulgaricum* × *G. reptans*) — Best in rock gardens. Does not tolerate heat or dry conditions. Flowers bright orange-scarlet. Plants 8 inches in height.
Sources: 4,13,32,49,66; C

G. 'Fire Opal' — 2½ to 3-inch brilliant red flowers with bronze overtones.
Sources: 13,32,66; C

G. 'Golden Sunset' — Semidouble golden-orange flowers.
Source: 67

G. 'Lady Stradheden' — Semidouble golden-yellow flowers.
Sources: 24,60,66,69; A,B,I,J,K,L

G. 'Lamb's Spectacular' — Bright golden-yellow flowers. Plants 8 inches in height.
Source: 32

G. 'Mrs. Bradshaw' — Semidouble scarlet flowers.
Sources: 3,24,49,59,60,67,69; A,B,I,J,K,L

G. 'Princess Juliana' — Semidouble, bronzy-orange flowers.
Sources: 13,32,66; C

G. 'Red Wings' — Semidouble scarlet flowers.
Source: 32

G. 'Starker's Magnificent' — Double apricot-orange flowers.
Sources: 24,32,66; I

G. 'Wilton Ruby' — Glowing ruby-red flowers.
Sources: 13; C

Gypsophila   **Baby's Breath, Chalk Plant**
                        Carnation Family (Caryophyllaceae)
The second common name and the generic name, derived from the Greek word which means lime-loving, give one of the main clues to success with this group. It is wise to have the soil tested before attempting to grow *Gypsophila*; if the reaction is lower than pH6, ground limestone should be applied to bring it up to pH7 or pH7.5. One other condition is equally as necessary if success is to be achieved: *Gypsophila* will not overwinter in moist soggy soils and a well-drained sunny situation is essential. Care should be taken in choosing a good location because all except the dwarf cultivars of Baby's Breath take up

[95]

a lot of room. Once established, they should not be moved as the thick fleshy roots resent disturbance.

These may seem rather exacting requirements for a plant that is included in a list of maintenance-free garden subjects. These requisites are, however, relatively simple if properly understood; and once established *Gypsophila* can be expected to grow for years with little further attention if it receives the necessary dose of ground limestone from time to time. A position in full sun is desirable, but light shade during part of the day is also acceptable. In our area it is wise to protect the plants with a winter mulch. This, however, should not cover the crown lest rotting occur before the ground becomes completely frozen.

G. paniculata — Baby's Breath — Single, white-flowered form. Plants grow to a height of 3 feet or more with a similar spread. In July masses of flowers are produced in large panicles. These are excellent for cutting and, if picked when fully open, are easily dried by placing the stems upside-down in a shady, well-ventilated place. This applies to cultivars of G. *paniculata* as well. Plants take at least two years to become established; spring planting is favored so they will have the benefit of an entire growing season before winter arrives.
Sources: 3,25,46; E,,J,K

G. paniculata 'Bristol Fairy' — The most popular, and perhaps the best cultivar. The double white flowers are freely produced in July and again in August to October if the old flowers are removed. It is a large plant; established specimens often will cover an area 4 feet wide. This and the other cultivars are grafted onto roots of G. *paniculata*, and it is advisable that the graft union be set at least 1 inch below the soil line. This will encourage roots from the stems and possibly help to keep them from flopping. Even so, the taller varieties often require staking as soon as the growth starts to appear. (See section on staking.)
Sources: 3,13,23,24,25,28,32,37,44,58,59,60,67,68,69; B,C,G,I, J,K,L

G. paniculata 'Compacta' — A smaller form with single white flowers. Plants 2 to 3 feet in height with a similar width.
Sources: 37,67

G. paniculata 'Compacta Plena' — Double white-flowered form of the preceding.
Sources: 13; C,H,L

Gypsophila paniculata 'Bristol Fairy' planted too close to a clump of Day-lilies.

G. paniculata 'Perfecta' — Double white flowers up to twice the size of those of G. 'Bristol Fairy'. Plants of compact habit, about 3 to 4 feet in height and up to 3 feet wide.
Sources: 3,7,24,32,67,69; I

G. repens — Creeping Baby's Breath — Trailing, nearly prostrate plants with 12 to 18-inch stems bearing masses of white flowers in early summer. Cultivars of this species are hardier than those of G. paniculata. Suited to the front of the border, but have many other uses in rock gardens or on dry walls.
Sources: 3,69; B,J,K

G. repens 'Rosea' — Rosy pink flowers. Plants about 6 inches.
Sources: 3,4,13,24,29,59,68,69; A,B,C,E,I,J,L

G. repens '**Rosy Veil**' (syn. 'Rosenschlier') — Delicate, double, soft pink to white clusters of flowers on interwoven stems; blooms June to August. Grows in an erect manner to a height of 18 inches. Due to the tangled stems, it is not good for cut flowers, but in all other respects is a fine border plant. Although commonly classed as a cultivar of *G. repens*, it may be a hybrid.
Sources: 3,24,32,59; H,I

G. × '**Bodgeri**' (*G. repens* 'Rosea' × *G. paniculata*) — Similar in overall appearance to cultivars of *G. paniculata* but considerably more compact. Semidouble white flowers, often with a pinkish tinge, in late May through June. Thoroughly hardy. Excellent for cut flowers.
Sources: 24,32,68; I

G. '**Pink Fairy**' — Usually offered as a cultivar of *G. paniculata*. Double pink flowers which are produced for most of the summer. Plants 18 inches to 2 feet in height.
Sources: 7,13,24,37,44,58,60,69; B,C,G,I,J,K,L

G. '**Pink Star**' — Usually offered as a cultivar of *G. paniculata*. Double pink flowers. Plants about 18 inches in height.
Sources: 25,28,32,67,68

> **G. oldhamiana** — Pale pink flowers in dense clusters in August and September. Plants about 3 feet in height. Not superior to any of the above, and inclined to flop.
> Sources: 4,46

> **G.** '**Flamingo**' — Double-flowered form which perhaps belongs to the above species. Flowers pink with tints of mauve.
> Sources: 13,24,59; C,I

Helenium
Sneezeweed, Helen's Flower
Daisy Family (Compositae)

Cultivars of our native *H. autumnale* have long been considered valuable for fall color in the border. Some cultivars grow from 4 to 6 feet tall and must be divided, if not every other year, then every third year, to maintain any semblance whatever of tidiness. The few available cultivars under 2½ feet may go for longer periods, and do not require staking as the taller ones do. For this reason they are useful in the low maintenance garden as a partial substitute for Chrysanthemums. They blossom throughout most of the late summer and autumn, with numerous small, Daisy-like flowers in shades ranging through yellow and red to bronze.

Helenium 'Butterpat' with underplanting of hardy Chrysanthemums.

A position in full sun is necessary. Plants perform poorly in dry soils; those of moderate fertility and high organic matter content will produce the best results. Sneezeweeds are remarkably tolerant of wet soil conditions during the growing season. Division to rejuvenate the plants should be done after the fourth year. The cultivars recommended here are best seen in groups of three planted 18 to 20 inches apart at the front or middle of the border.

H. autumnale 'Brilliant' — The tallest variety recommended. About 3 feet in height with strong stems.
Source: 69

H. autumnale 'Moerheim Beauty' — Deep bronze-red flowers in July and August. Plants 2½ feet in height.
Sources: 13; C

H. hoopsei — Orange Sneezeweed — Unlike the cultivars of *H. autumnale*, this species blooms in May and June with large orange flowers. It will tolerate light shade. Plants 2 feet in height.
Sources: E,L

H. autumnale 'Pumilum Magnificum' — Deep yellow flowers from late July through September on plants 12 to 18 inches tall.
Sources: 32,67

> *H. autumnale* — 4 to 6 feet under garden conditions. Flowers yellow.
> Sources: 14,39
> *H.* 'Bruno' — Flowers deep mahogany-red in August and September. Plants up to 4 feet high.
> Sources: 25,66,67; K
> *H.* 'Butterpat' — Flowers yellow. Plants 3 to 4 feet in height.
> Sources: 13,25,66,67,68,69; C,K
> *H.* 'Chippersfield Orange' — Flowers copper to gold with markings of crimson. Plants 4 feet in height.
> Source: 67

Heliopsis   **Heliopsis, Hardy Zinnia, Orange Sunflower**
                     Daisy Family (Compositae)

At the middle or rear of the border, these plants are of value for their bright color and long blooming season. Semidouble or double bright yellow to orange flowers which are up to 3 to 4 inches across appear in midsummer and fall and are excellent for cutting. Plants are usually 3 feet in height, with strong stems which do not topple.

About the only requirements are a position in full sun and soil that is moderately rich and does not dry out during the summer months. During periods of drought, frequent irrigation is advisable. If one's soil conditions are poor and dry, it probably would be better to avoid this group.

H. 'Golden Plume' ('Goldgefieder') — Bright yellow, nearly 3-inch flowers which are almost fully double; the centers are greenish. June to September. Plants 3 to 3½ feet in height.
Sources: 24; I

H. 'Gold Greenheart' — Completely double bright yellow flowers with emerald-green centers. As the flowers age, the green disappears. Plants 3 feet in height.
Sources: 13,68,69; C

H. 'Hohlspiegel' — 4-inch golden-yellow, semidouble flowers. July to September. Plants 3 feet in height.
Source: 69

H. scabra 'Incomparabilis' — Deep yellow semidouble flowers with dark centers and overlapping petals. Plants 3 feet in height.
Sources: 32,60,66,67,69; L

H. 'Karat' — Single deep yellow flowers. Plants 4 feet in height.
Source: 69

H. 'Summer Sun' — Double golden yellow flowers. Plants 3 feet in height.
Sources: 13,24,67; A,C,I,K

Helleborous   Hellebore
Buttercup Family (Ranunculaceae)
Depending upon weather conditions and species selected, this is a small group of perennial plants which will bloom anytime from about mid-November to May. The Christmas Rose, *H. niger* has a time span between November and April in periods when the ground is free of snow. The Lenten Rose, *H. orientalis* and its cultivars are later, from about early March to May. The exact timing depends upon weather and may vary from year to year.

The use of the word "Rose" in the common names may be misleading. These are not shrubs, but true herbaceous perennials about 15 inches in height with lustrous, leathery, dark evergreen leaves. The flowers are borne several to a stem and vary between 2 and 5 inches in diameter. The five large petal-like sepals surround a conspicuous center of yellow stamens.

These are plants which should be seen at close range to be fully appreciated; moreover, because of the time of the year in which they flower, a location close to a walk, patio, or a prominent part of the perennial or shrub border should be chosen. An area where the plants will receive partial shade in the summer and some sun in winter is best. The soil should be well drained, but not dry; this usually will necessitate the addition of organic matter. Highly acid soils are unsatisfactory and should be limed to bring the pH to around 6.5 or 7. Hellebores will benefit from the addition of about a handful of ground limestone around each plant every third or fourth year.

If the above conditions can be provided, culture is simple, and the plants will be very long-lived. They resent disturbance and take several years to form sizeable clumps. Spring is the best time for planting and the crown should be covered with about an inch of soil. A mulch is recommended to keep the plants evenly moist during the summer months, and irrigation will be necessary in times of drought. The life of the flowers can be prolonged by covering the plants with a small frame of plastic which is open at the base or ends to allow free circulation of air. This will help to keep ice and snow from the blossoms and prevent mud from being splashed onto them. The flowers are excellent for cutting and most valuable considering the time when they are in bloom. Char the base of the stems with a flame immediately after cutting.

H. niger — Christmas Rose, Black Hellebore — The Latin name and the second common name refer to the black roots, not the flowers. The latter are white, faintly flushed with pink as they age, and borne one to three per stem. They may vary between 2 and 4 inches in diameter. The leaf margins have sparse, coarse teeth.
Sources: 13,23,24,32,59,66,67,68,69; C,I,L

H. niger var. *altifolius* — A very desirable variety. The flowers are larger, up to 5 inches across, on stems an inch or 2 taller than those of the species.
Sources: 30,32,60

H. orientalis — Lenten Rose — A very variable species. Flowers are 2 to 3 inches in diameter and come in shades from white to chocolate-brown, purple, and rarely green. The leaves are a paler green and the margins bear numerous small serrated teeth.
Sources: 59,66

***H. orientalis* 'Atrorubens'** — The petals are chocolate-purple on the inside, and greenish and purple on the outside. Said to be easier to transplant than other varieties.
Sources: 13,24,67; C,I

***H. orientalis* 'Millet Hybrids'** — A group having 2 to 3-inch flowers in colors ranging from pure white, to pink, red, and chocolate. Some are speckled and striped.
Source: 32

Hemerocallis   **Daylily**
Lily Family (Liliaceae)

Hybridizers have produced so many cultivars of this nearly-perfect plant for the low maintenance garden that the greatest problem is knowing which varieties to choose. In general, the plants are nearly indestructible if placed in a reasonably fertile soil in sun or partial shade; excessive fertility will lead to rank growth and poor flowering. Soils which are fairly well supplied with organic matter and do not remain soggy for long periods will produce best results. Planting is best done in the spring at distances of about 2 feet to allow for expansion of the clumps. Although Daylilies have the reputation of being able to remain nearly forever without being divided, the most vigorous, heavy-flowering clumps are obtained when the plants are divided at intervals of four to six years. About the only other work is the removal of the flower stems once the blossoms have faded. These present rather an ugly appearance if left to dry on the plants.

Daylilies now can be obtained in almost any color of the rainbow; some varieties often combine two or more colors or hues. Flowers range in size from 3 to 8 inches across and may have a single ring of petals, or a double row of overlapping petals. When plants are in bloom, heights may range from about 20 inches to 4 or 5 feet according to variety. With careful selection it is now possible to obtain a flowering span from May to October.

Above: Hemerocallis — *An unnamed hybrid seedling growing in a suburban Boston garden.*

Right: Hemerocallis 'First Choice'

Much attention is presently given by *Hemerocallis* fanciers to a relatively new group called the tetraploids. These are varieties whose chromosome numbers have been doubled and, in general, are more robust and have larger flowers than the standard or diploid varieties. At present, the former fall into the category of "collectors items" due to their relative scarcity and very high prices ($100.00 and frequently much more is not an uncommon price for a newly-introduced tetraploid cultivar.) Ordinary gardeners will want to select from the more reasonably priced diploids.

Many hundreds of varieties are listed by nurseries, and there are many nurseries which specialize in *Hemerocallis* exclusively. It would be very difficult to choose the best moderately priced varieties to grow today if it were not for the Popularity Poll published in the December issue of the *Hemerocallis Journal*. Daylily fanciers throughout the country have sent in lists of what they consider the best cultivars.

The following eight cultivars received the largest number of votes in the New England Region in December 1973. These are listed in order of popularity:

H. 'Mary Todd' — Large 6-inch, ruffled, golden-yellow flowers with very wide petals. 24 to 26 inches in height. Tetraploid.
Sources: 35,54,66

H. 'Winning Ways' — 6 to 8-inch greenish-yellow flowers with green throats. Wide, overlapping petals. 32 to 34 inches in height. Diploid.
Sources: 54,56,66; M

H. 'Catherine Woodberry' — Delicate 6-inch, light orchid flowers with green throats. 30 inches in height. Diploid.
Sources: 56,66

H. 'Hortensia' — 5-inch medium yellow, waxy flowers with ruffled, crimped borders. Greenish-yellow throats. 34 inches in height. Diploid.
Sources: 40,66; M

H. 'Cherry Cheeks' — 6-inch pinkish-red flowers with small yellow throats. Quite velvety in texture. 28 to 30 inches in height. Tetraploid.
Sources: 56,66

H. 'Heavenly Harp' — Polychrome type of flower, basically creamy-yellow overlaid with gold, and with bright pink ribs and a flush of intense rose-pink at the tips of the petals. Very ruffled. 28 to 32 inches in height. Tetraploid.
Sources: 35,40,56,66; M

H. 'Ice Carnival' — Icy and crisp, near-white, 6-inch flowers with small green throats. 28 inches in height. Diploid.
Sources: 54,66; M

H. 'Little Wart' — Attractive deep lavender-purple, 3½-inch flowers with green throats. 18 to 24 inches in height. Diploid.
Sources: 35,54,61

Other cultivars well suited to our area, which ranked high in the national polls are as follows:

H. 'Little Rainbow' — Polychrome blend of colors. Basically creamy-yellow overlaid with hues of bright pink. 26 inches in height. Diploid.
Sources: 40,54,56,66

H. 'Renee' — Clear, pale yellow, 3½-inch flowers which are nearly circular in form. Small green throats. 28 inches in height. Diploid.
Sources: 40,55; M

H. 'Perennial Pleasure' — Bright yellow, 6-inch ruffled flowers. Fragrant and remain open into the evening. 26 inches in height. Diploid.
Sources: 54,66

H. 'Lavender Flight' — 6¼-inch deep lavender flowers with ruffled, wide petals, yellowish-green throats. Hold color well in hot sun. 34 inches in height. Diploid.
Sources: 35; M

H. 'Sail On' — Bright red flowers of very firm substance. 30 to 34 inches in height. Diploid.
Source: 66

Heuchera   **Coral Bells, Alum Root**
                              Saxifrage Family (Saxifragaceae)

These are excellent plants with few troubles, and capable of being left in place at least five years or longer before division will perform well in light shade. Soil should be well drained both in summer and winter, but should have sufficient humus so that it does not dry out quickly in the summer. Despite their long, fleshy roots, plants are very subject to being heaved out of the ground during periods of alternate freezing and thawing in late winter. To help alleviate this, the crowns should be set an inch below the soil level and mulching is advisable. Because of the heaving tendency, spring planting is preferred so that as large a root system as possible will be produced before winter. Divide only when the clumps become old and woody and flower production is scanty.

Heucheras produce numerous dainty, pendent, bell-shaped flowers on stems 15 inches to 2½ feet. Colors range from white to pink and vivid deep red. The blossoming period in June and July can be prolonged somewhat by removing the faded flower stalks and watering during dry periods. Flowers are excellent for cutting. The leaves are evergreen, and in some cultivars they are marbled with patches of bronze.

The modern cultivars are mainly derived from crossing *H. sanguinea* and some of its cultivars with *H. micrantha*. Although several of the species are offered in catalogs, all the cultivars are superior in flower. Approximately 30 named cultivars are being offered in this country at the present time; the following is but a selection:

H. '**Bressingham Hybrids**' — A strain of mixed colors in shades from white to pink to coral-red in May. Flowers stems 2 feet in height.
Sources: 24,32,67; A,B,I

H. '**Brizoides**' — Small, soft pink flowers on stems 20 to 24 inches in height.
Sources: 13; C,J,L

H. '**Chartreuse**' — Flowers soft chartreuse, an unusual color in this group. Stems about 20 inches in height.
Source: 67

H. '**Chatterbox**' — Deep rose-pink flowers. Stems 18 inches in height.
Sources: 24,49,66; I,J,K

H. '**Fire Sprite**' — Large rose-red flowers.
Source: 67

H. 'Freedom' — Rose-pink flowers. Stems 18 inches in height.
Sources: 32,67,68

H. 'June Bride' — Large pure white flowers on 15-inch stems.
Source: 67

H. 'Peachblow' — Pink flowers tipped with white.
Source: 32

H. 'Pluie de Feu' — Cherry-red flowers on stems about 18 inches
high.
Sources: 3,24,68,69; I,L

H. 'Rosamundi' — Probably the best coral-pink variety for those
who wish Coral Bells. Stems 15 to 18 inches in height.
Sources: 3,13,23,24,66,67; C,I

H. 'Scarlet Sentinel' — Large scarlet-red flowers on strong 24 to
30-inch stems. Very showy in flower.
Sources: 29,32,66

H. 'Snowflakes' — Large white flowers.
Sources: 3,32

H. 'Splendens' — Bright scarlet-red flowers on 28-inch stems.
Sources: 4,24,68; A,I

H. 'White Cloud' — Flowers white to cream in color on 18-inch
stems.
Sources: 13,24,49,69; C,I,J,L

Hibiscus   **Hardy Hibiscus, Rose Mallow**
Hibiscus Family (Malvaceae)

    The numerous cultivars which have arisen from the selection
and crossing of *H. moscheutos* and *H. palustris* are not frequently seen in the Boston area even though most of them are perfectly hardy. This is strange because the equally showy, tropical representatives of this genus, so frequently associated with
Florida or Hawaii, are featured in many amateur greenhouses.
    Some of the new cultivars display gigantic flowers up to 10
and 12 inches across, making them the largest flowered herbaceous perennials that can be grown in this area. Some people
object to the size and bright colors as being too gaudy; but when
plants are grown as single specimens in the mixed border, striking effects can be achieved. The largest flowers are produced

Foliage of Heuchera sanguinea

[109]

at the beginning of the blooming season in midsummer. By fall the flowers are usually smaller by about 2 inches.

Hardy Hibiscus are of very easy culture. They are the perfect answer to locations that are too moist for most other herbaceous perennials to survive; conversely, they will grow perfectly well in an ordinary well-drained garden soil. In moist areas heights may range from 5 to 8 feet, but in drier soils 3 to 5 feet is about average, depending on cultivar. Full sun is preferred. These are quite long-lived plants that resent disturbance. About their only fault is that the flowers are attractive to Japanese Beetles. It is fortunate that the blossoming period of most of the varieties extends well after the worst of the beetle population is gone. In wet areas self-seeding may occur freely, and if the named varieties are to be perpetuated, it would be best to remove all seedlings.

Hibiscus 'White Beauty'

Hibiscus 'Appleblossom' attacked by Japanese Beetles.

Some nurseries list a selection of unnamed varieties under such names as Mallow Marvels Mixed or Giant Mix. The following sources are for named varieties only:

H. 'Albino' — Flowers pure white.
Source: 37

H. 'Appleblossom' — Flowers light pink margined with deeper rose-pink. Crinkly petals.
Sources: 2,66

H. 'Brilliant' — Flowers bright red.
Source: 37

H. 'Cotton Candy' — Flowers soft pink.
Source: 67

H. 'Crimson Wonder' — Flowers rich red.
Sources: 60,66,67; M

H. 'Intense Pink' — Flowers rose-pink, brighter pink veins.
Sources: 67; M

H. **'Pink Giant'** — Flowers large pale pink with a small red throat.
Source: 67

H. **'Pink Princess'** — Flowers clear pink.
Source: 37

H. **'Raspberry Rose'** — Flowers deep rose-pink with a bright red throat.
Source: 2

H. **'Ruby Dot'** — Flowers white with a ruby-red throat.
Sources: 60,67

H. **'Ruffled White'** — Smaller than usual. White flowers with a crimson throat. Petals crinkly at the edges.
Source: 2

H. **'Satan'** — Large brilliant fire engine-red flowers.
Sources: 2,23,66,67

H. **'Snow White'** — Flowers pure white with a cream throat.
Sources: 23,67

H. **'Strawberry Blonde'** — Flowers bright deep pink, not as large as some of the others.
Source: 67

H. **'Super Clown'** — Very large creamy-white flowers shaded rose-pink.
Sources: 2; M

H. **'Super Red'** — Medium size dark red flowers.
Source: 2

H. **'Super Rose'** — Flowers rose-pink.
Sources: 23,48,60; M

Hosta   **Plantain-lily, Hosta, Funkia**
                                 Lily Family (Liliaceae)
If given a proper location as regards both soil and light, this group can rank high amongst those to delight the gardener who cannot spend a lot of time pampering his plants. A moderately rich soil with partial shade (preferably the shade of high trees) is about all that Hostas require to develop into majestic, eye-catching specimens. They will survive in almost any

Hosta Collection of the Arnold Arboretum at the Case Estates in Weston, Mass. Photo: P. Bruns.

type of soil, but are best in one well-supplied with organic matter. Wet soil conditions should be avoided.

A visit to the Hosta collection at the Case Estates of the Arnold Arboretum can be a rewarding experience for most visitors are unaware of the exciting range of variations in the group. This special planting is one of the most extensive collections of Hostas in this part of the country.

The most demanding seasonal task with Hostas is the removal of the flower stems once the blooming period has finished. They not only are unattractive when they dry out, but should not be allowed to go to seed; most named varieties do not reproduce true to type and the resulting seedlings can be a distinct nuisance. Nonetheless some of the best cultivars on the market today have arisen as chance seedlings in just this way.

There is little doubt that most *Hosta* cultivars are seen to best advantage if planted singly as specimen plants rather than being massed. In this way the handsome radial symmetry of the individual plants can be appreciated. Some of the more vigorous varieties will eventually occupy up to 3 to 4 feet of space in the garden and this must be taken into account at planting time. Some types make excellent ground covers, but the symmetrical effect is sacrificed. *H. undulata* with its white and green wavy leaves has been used extensively for this purpose, perhaps overly so, and is often seen growing in the full sun — a condition not tolerated well by most other species.

The taxonomy of *Hosta* is confused, and synonyms and incorrect names abound in the trade. The following is a selection of the many varieties offered. It should be noted here that they fall into two different groups: some grown for the interesting leaves only, and others for their flowers as well. If the latter are of primary interest, choices from this list will provide a period of blossom from late June into September.

H. albomarginata (syn. *H. lancifolia* var. *albo-marginata*) — White Rim Plantain-lily — This is a rather small plant. Clumps spread to about 2 feet. Leaves lance-shaped, with very narrow, pure white borders sometimes marked by short stripes running toward the center. Flowers are pale lilac on stems about 2 feet in height. Blooms in August.
Sources: 7,20,21,24,32,51,67,68; B,I,J

H. decorata (syn. *H.* 'Thomas Hogg') — Blunt Plantain-lily — Similar to *H. albomarginata* in size and leaf coloration. Leaves are oval with blunt tips, about 6 inches long, with a prominent

silvery margin. Flowers are dark lilac on 2-foot stems; August blooming. Plants form 2-foot mounds.
Sources: 3,7,13,21,32,46,49,51,58,61,66,67; C

H. fortunei —Fortune's Plantain-lily — Leaves are 5 to 8 inches long, pale green and quite glaucous. Flowers are white to lavender, almost 1½ inches long, on 3-foot stems in August.
Sources: 7,21,24,51,66,67,69; J

H. fortunei var. **gigantea** — A very large form of the preceding species with leaves up to 12 inches. Mature clumps may reach up to 5 feet in diameter and are just the thing for a really bold accent.
Sources: 51,61,66

H. fortunei 'Marginata-alba' — Irregular shiny white bands around the leaf edges.
Sources: 7,61

H. fortunei 'Marginata-aurea' — Yellow borders on the leaves.
Sources: 24,61; I

Overleaf top left: Hosta plantaginea

Bottom left: Hosta sieboldiana 'Frances Williams'

Top right: Hosta sieboldiana

Bottom right: An effective grouping of Hostas illustrating their diversity of texture, leaf form, and flower.

H. lancifolia — Narrow-leaved or Japanese Plantain-lily — 6-inch-long lance-shaped leaves forming dense clumps about 2 feet across. Pale lilac flowers on 2-foot stems in August.
Sources: 13,21,24,49,51,61,68,69; B,C,I,J,L

H. plantaginea (syn. *H. subcordata, H. grandiflora*) — Fragrant Plantain-lily — Grown especially for the flowers which are white and trumpet-like up to 4 inches long. These appear in late August and September on 2-foot stems and are very fragrant. Clumps grow to a width of 3 feet. Shiny, rounded, pale green leaves.
Sources: 7,13,21,23,32,46,51,61,66,67,68; C,L

H. sieboldiana (syn. *H. glauca*) — Blue-leaved or Siebold Plantain-lily — The species and its cultivars are grown for the remarkably large, heavy-textured leaves, often crinkled somewhat like seersucker. The leaves are gray-green with a bluish cast; usually up to 12 inches in length. The flowers are white, appear in July and are usually pretty much hidden amongst the foliage. Plants develop into clumps about a yard in width.
Sources: 3,4,7,13,21,32,49,51,59,61,66,67,68; C,J,L

H. sieboldiana 'Frances Williams' (syn. *H. sieboldiana* 'Yellow Edge' or *H. sieboldiana aureo-marginata*) — One of the most desirable of all cultivars. The rounded glaucous leaves are bordered in shades of cream and yellow.
Sources: 7,21,32,51,61,66

H. tardiflora (syn. *H. lancifolia* var. *tardiflora*) — Autumn Plantain-lily — Of interest for its very late deep lavender-purple flowers in October. The plants are quite diminutive for the group, only 12 inches wide at maximum with a similar height.
Sources: 7,32,61,66

H. undulata (syn. *H. media picta, H. variegata*) — Wavyleaf Plantain-lily — The leaves have wavy margins and are variegated white on green. The flowers appear in July on 3-inch stems and are pale lavender. Plants are about 20 inches in width. This is the species that is perhaps the most familiar, having been used extensively as an edging plant for borders and walks. Withstands conditions in full sun better than the others.
Sources: 3,7,12,13,20,23,24,28,30,32,46,51,59,61,66,67,68; A,B,C,I,L

H. undulata var. *univittata* (syn. *H. univittata*) — The large green, waxy leaves have a central white stripe. The flowers are clear lavender and appear in July.
Sources: 7,21,51,61,66

H. ventricosa (syn. *H. coerulea*) — Blue Plantain-lily — The large, shiny, deep green leaves are twisted at the tips. The large flowers appear on 3-foot stems in July and August and are near-blue with a purplish tinge. Clumps reach a width of about 2 feet.
Sources: 4,7,13,21,51,57,61,66,67,69; B,C,H

H. 'Betsy King' — Grown mainly for its rich purple flowers on 20-inch stems in August.
Sources: 51,61

H. 'Honeybells' (*H. lancifolia* × *H. plantaginea*) — Very fragrant medium-sized lilac-lavender flowers striped blue on 3-foot stems in August.
Sources: 3,7,13,20,21,24,28,32,49,51,61,68,69; B,C,F,G,I,J,L

H. 'Royal Standard' — Very sweetly scented white flowers on 2-foot stems in August and September.
Sources: 24,59,61,61; I

Iberis   Candytuft
                                   Mustard Family (Cruciferae)
    Evergreen mounds of shiny foliage up to 2 feet wide covered with masses of white flowers in May characterize this valuable group for the low maintenance border. Cutting back the old stems at least halfway after the flowers have gone by is about the only work necessary. This will promote vigorous new growth and prevent the clumps from becoming woody and open-centered. A light, well-drained soil is necessary. Wet soil conditions in the winter lessen the hardiness of most varieties. In open winters without much snow, a light covering of evergreen boughs will prevent the foliage from burning. Aside from these few simple requirements, Candytufts present few other demands and will thrive for many years. In the perennial garden they should be planted in groups of at least three spaced about 15 inches apart so the clumps will grow together at their edges.

I. sempervirens — Evergreen Candytuft — The most common species offered, and the most reliable in the Northeast. Numerous pure white clusters of flowers are borne on 8-inch stems in May. Older plants will form mounds 6 to 9 inches high and as much as 2 feet in diameter.
Sources: 3,13,14,23,24,25,39,46,66,67,68; A,C,E,I,J,K,L

I. sempervirens **'Autumn Snow'** — Blooms again in September. Fairly compact habit of growth.
Sources: 13,28,44,65,66,67,68; C

I. sempervirens **'Little Gem'** — Compact plants only 6 inches high and 8 inches in diameter with small leaves and small clusters of flowers.
Sources: 3,13,24,66,68; C,I

I. sempervirens **'Purity'** — Quite compact habit of growth, but somewhat larger than the preceding cultivar. Very free blooming, flowers pure white.
Sources: 3,13,24,67,68,69; C,I,J,L

I. sempervirens **'Snowflake'** — Forms mounds 8 to 10 inches high with heavy foliage and large white flowers.
Sources: 13,24,32,59,66,68; C,I

I. sempervirens **'Snowmantle'** — Forms mounds about 8 inches high and is of quite compact growth.
Sources: 13,28,66; C,G,J,K,L

> *I. gibraltarica* — Gibraltar Candytuft — Not fully hardy in our area. Plants of a rather scraggly habit, but with handsome lilac to light purple flowers which are produced into July.
> Source: 49

> *I. tenoreana* — Tenore Candytuft — Not fully hardy in our area, growth too unpredictable.
> Source: 32

Iris

Iris, Fleur-de-lis
Iris Family (Iridaceae)

There are so many varieties of Iris from which to choose that one hardly knows where to begin. The Tall, Intermediate, and Dwarf groups of Bearded Irises, which are the most popular groups grown, are the most demanding. The Siberian Irises, especially, and to a lesser extent the Japanese Irises, are not so demanding. Each group is discussed separately in order of their desirability for the low maintenance garden.

I. sibirica — Siberian Iris — The easiest type of Iris to grow in our area; forms large clumps up to 3 feet tall, with slender leaves, and 3-inch flowers in shades from white through blue and deep blue, purple, reddish-purple and violet. The blooming season is from mid-June to early July, just after the Bearded Irises and before the Japanese Irises. This species is fairly undemanding as to soil conditions, and although the plants will tolerate a somewhat poor dry soil, performance always will be best on rich, moist, slightly acid soils. They are best in full sun, but will tolerate partial shade as well. Very little attention is necessary. After a number of years the clumps will have started to die out at the center and division must be resorted to. It is fortunate that this is an infrequent task, as the large clumps are deeply rooted and become so tightly matted together at the base that the lifting and dividing process can be quite arduous. Planting and division are best done in the spring.

Siberian Irises present a far different picture in the garden than the more familiar Bearded Irises do. The foliage is more refined and the sizeable clumps have an upright vase-shaped habit of growth. When used singly scattered here and there from the front to middle of the border, they provide excellent bold contrasts. Although the range of flower colors and the length of the flowering season are considerably more limited than those of Bearded Irises, the foliage effect alone makes Siberian Iris worthy of consideration in any garden. When blossoming has finished, the numerous flower stalks bear attractive 2 to 3-inch seed pods. These dry out and turn brown later in the season, and are very handsome if left on the plants through the winter. They also are attractive in winter arrangements.

I. sibirica **'Cambridge'** — Large turquoise-blue flowers.
Sources: 48,52,69

I. sibirica **'Caesar's Brother'** — Deep pansy-purple flowers.
Sources: 13,21,24,38,49,67,69; B,C,I,K,L,M

I. sibirica **'Eric the Red'** — Reddish-purple flowers.
Sources: 13,38,48; C

I. sibirica **'Gatineau'** — Large violet-blue flowers.
Sources: 21,38,48

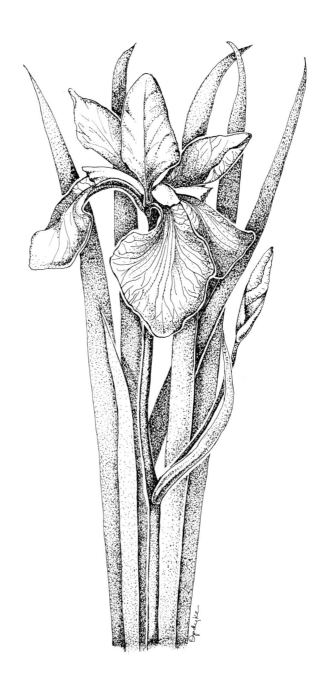

I. sibirica 'Perry's Pygmy' — Deep blue, plants only 20 inches high.
Sources: 21,48,69

I. sibirica 'Ruby Wine' — Bright ruby-red flowers.
Sources: 38,48,52

I. sibirica 'Sea Shadows' — Flowers mixed blue and turquoise.
Sources: 48,52,69

I. sibirica 'Snow Crest' — Ruffled white flowers.
Sources: 21,48,66

I. sibirica 'Tycoon' — Large deep violet-blue flowers.
Sources: 21,25,38,48,67,68

I. sibirica 'Violet Repeat' — Bright violet flowers which are often produced intermittently after the main blooming season.
Sources: 48,52,69

I. sibirica 'White Swirl' — Satin white flowers produced in abundance.
Sources: 21,38,48,52,66,69

I. sibirica 'White Magnificence' — Large white flowers.
Sources: 38,48,52

Iris kaempferi — Japanese Iris — Members of this group are far more demanding than Siberian Iris as to soil conditions, but if the proper site can be provided, they are easy to grow and have few problems. It would be wise to avoid them altogether, however, if one's soil conditions do not approximate the following: quite acid, rich, and capable of retaining abundant moisture throughout the growing season. Anything else usually will produce inferior results. Full sun or partial shade is satisfactory. If lime is spread anywhere near the plants, fatalities quickly occur.

Given the above requirements, Japanese Irises have few problems and can be left alone without disturbance for many years. They are ideal for planting at the edges of ponds and streams, or in the border if the soil is moist. The leaves are narrow, like the Siberian Irises. The plants grow to a height of $2\frac{1}{2}$ to 3 feet with flowering stems 3 to 4 feet tall. The large, 6-inch, flat-topped, beardless flowers come in shades of white, blue, rose, and purple, often with attractive combinations of color. Spring is the recommended planting time.

I. kaempferi 'Great White Heron' — Semidouble, large, pure white flowers.
Sources: 66,69

Iris sibirica — *Siberian Iris*

I. kaempferi 'Jeweled Kimona' — Flowers white with blue markings.
Source: 68

I. kaempferi 'Kagari Bi' — Large rose-pink flowers.
Sources: 21,24,69; I

I. kaempferi 'Mahogany' — Double deep red flowers.
Sources: 21,24,68; I

I. kaempferi 'Pink Frost' — Double light pink flowers to 8 inches across.
Sources: 21,69

I. kaempferi 'Pin Stripe' — Flowers white, penciled with bright blue stripes.
Sources: 66,69

I. kaempferi 'Purple and Gold' — Velvety purple flowers with golden throats.
Sources: 21,68,69

I. kaempferi 'Rose Anna' — Flowers mauve, veined with rich purple.
Sources: 21,24,68; I

Bearded Iris — Although these rank high on the popularity list in perennial gardens, they have several serious faults and cannot be recommended for most low maintenance situations. Division or reduction in size of the clump every third or fourth year is necessary to prevent deterioration and to maintain vigor. This process involves separating the rhizomes, specialized stems that creep near the surface of the ground, and replanting them about an inch below soil level in groups of three. The foliage, hence the new growth, should face outward; the leaves are cut back to about 6 inches. This usually is done as soon as flowering has finished; however, satisfactory results are obtained any time up to August.

The most serious problem with Bearded Iris is their susceptibility to attack by the Iris Borer. This is a worm which tunnels into the rhizome via the leaves. Aside from the damage the borer does to the plants, it opens the way to a bacterial infection known as Soft Rot. This is a foul-smelling rot which can infect the entire rhizome.

Control of borers and Soft Rot often necessitates digging up and discarding (burning) the affected rhizomes. In the autumn it is prudent to remove and burn old foliage on which borer eggs may overwinter. Systemic insecticides such as Cygon sprayed as the leaves begin to grow, and again just before flowering, will effectively prevent borer infestations. Elimination of the borers is the most effective prevention for the Soft Rot disease.

Bearded Irises are obtained in nearly every color, in fact the genus name *Iris* is the Greek word for rainbow. Tall Bearded

Irises bear flowers up to 8 inches across on stems 3 to 4 feet in height. Intermediate Bearded Irises range in height from about 15 to 24 inches with 2 to 4-inch flowers. Dwarf Bearded Irises are under 10 inches in height with 2 to 4-inch flowers. The Dwarf Bearded Irises appear to be less susceptible to borer problems than the other two groups.

Many hundreds of varieties are currently offered. Numerous nurseries specialize in *Iris* to the exclusion of all other plants. A large and flourishing society (The American Iris Society) devotes itself to the genus. As with the American Hemerocallis Society, a popularity poll is published yearly in the *Bulletin of the American Iris Society*. The following 12 Tall Bearded Irises are listed, in order of popularity, from the 1973 Poll of the 100 favorites:

I. 'Stepping Out' — Flowers white with violet margins.
Sources: 8,10,13,16,19,28,36,38,52,55,56,65,66,68,69; C,M

I. 'New Moon' — Large, ruffled, light yellow flowers.
Sources: 10,11,16,36,38,41,52,56,65; M

I. 'Babbling Brook' — Ruffled blue flowers with light textured veining, pale lemon-yellow beard.
Sources: 10,16,19,36,38,41,52,55,56,65,69; M

I. 'Debby Rairdon' — Excellent combination of white and soft yellow.
Sources: 10,16,19,36,38,52,55,56,65; M

I. 'Shipshape' — Intense medium blue.
Sources: 10,11,16,36,41,52,56,65; M

I. 'Pink Taffeta' — Heavily ruffled, light rose-pink.
Sources: 10,11,38,41,52,56,65; M

I. 'Dusky Dancer' — Very dark, velvety black-violet.
Sources: 10,11,16,19,36,38,41,52,56,65; M

I. 'Kilt Lilt' — Large flowers basically a blend of rich apricot and gold. Very ruffled.
Sources: 10,11,16,41,52,56,65; M

I. 'Cup Race' — Large, pure white flowers.
Sources: 10,16,19,28,38,41,52,65,69

I. 'Camelot Rose' — Large ruffled flowers. Combination of silky-textured orchid and bright burgundy-red.
Sources: 10,11,16,19,36,41,52,55,65,69; M

L. 'Lime Fiz' — Flowers shaded lime to pure yellow.
Sources: 10,11,16,41,52,65,69; M

I. 'Winter Olympics' — Large ruffled flowers of leathery substance. Pure white.
Sources: 10,16,19,36,38,52,55,65,69; M

Kniphofia

Torch-Lily, Red-Hot Poker, Tritoma
Lily Family (Liliaceae)

Although newer cultivars are, in general, hardier than the older ones, Torch-Lilies do not survive some Boston winters and cannot be recommended for general use here. *Kniphofia uvaria* (often listed in catalogs as *K. pfitzeri*), is the best known, commonly offered species, but its bright red and yellow flowers are thought to be overly gaudy by many people. This shortcoming has been remedied in the modern cultivars through breeding and selection which has produced a much better range of softer colors.

All Torch-Lilies require rich, perfectly drained soils. Soggy conditions are fatal, and although a position sheltered from the wind should be selected, they should be in a location which receives full sun for most of the day. Divisions obtained from nurseries are usually small and take a few years to become fully established. Spring is the only time for planting or dividing. After five or more years, clumps may build up to 2½ to 3 feet in width; however, division will not be necessary for many years.

Torch-Lilies range in height, according to variety, from 2 to 4 feet when in blossom. The individual drooping flowers are tubular and arranged in dense poker-like racemes at the tops of the flowering stems. The long, rigid leaves are somewhat grasslike in appearance. These are bold plants in flower and are suitable either as single specimens or in groupings of not more than three placed 15 to 18 inches apart either near the front or middle of the border.

Kniphofia is frequently listed by the old name *Tritoma* in catalogs.

K. **'Alcazar'** — Velvety textured rosy-red flowers. 3 feet.
Source: 44

K. **'Blastoff'** — Flowers pure white, red at the top of the spike. 3 feet.
Source: 7

K. **'Comet'** — Flowers orange-red. 2½ feet.
Sources: 7,24; I

K. **'Earliest of All'** — Flowers coral-rose. Blooms earlier than most other cultivars and is one of the hardiest. 2 to 2½ feet.
Source: 67

K. **'Glow'** — Flowers coral-red. 2½ feet.
Sources: 24,32; I

K. **'Golden Scepter'** — Deep yellow flowers. 3 feet.
Sources: 44,67

K. **'Goldmine'** — Burnished golden-yellow flowers. 3 feet.
Sources: 7,67; L

K. **'Maid of Orleans'** — Dense spikes of pale yellow flowers which fade quickly to a beautiful ivory-white. 3 to 3½ feet.
Source: 67

K. 'Primrose Beauty' — Primrose-yellow flowers. 2½ feet.
Sources: 7,13,24,32,66; C,I,K,L

K. 'Robin Hood' — Bright orange-scarlet flowers. 2 feet.
Sources: 13,44; C

K. 'Rosea Superba' — Flowers on the lower ⅔ of the stem are pure white; on the upper ⅓, pinkish-red. 2 feet.
Source: 67

K. 'Royal Standard' — Top flowers bright red; bottom, yellow-shaded to cream. 3 feet.
Sources: 24,66; I,L

K. 'Springtime' — Flowers on lower ½ of stem are ivory-white; those on top, bright coral-red.
Sources: 13,32,44,67; C

K. 'Vanilla' — Flowers clear pale yellow. 2 feet.
Source: 67

K. 'White Giant' — Flowers ivory-white, 3 feet.
Sources: 13,24,32,44,66; C,I,L

K. nelsonii var. major — A dwarf species with deep orange-scarlet flowers. 2 feet.
Source: 67

K. uvaria (syn. *K. pfitzeri*) — The typical old-fashioned form of Red-Hot Poker with scarlet upper flowers and yellow lower flowers. 3 feet.
Sources: 44,66; A,J,K,L

Liatris   **Blazing Star, Gayfeather, Button Snakeroot
                          Daisy Family (Compositae)**

It is rather unusual that a member of the Daisy family should have flowers which are arranged in a dense spike formation. It is also unusual for flower spikes to start blooming from the top and continue downward, but most all *Liatris* do this. The exceptions are *L. scariosa* 'September Glory', and its sport, *L. scariosa* 'White Spire'. These open their flowers more or less simultaneously. All the commonly grown species provide excellent flowers for cutting purposes, but these two are probably the best.

Liatris are upright plants which appear best when planted sparingly rather than as large masses. They will tolerate considerable moisture during the growing season, but soggy soil conditions during the winter will lead to rapid deterioration of the clumps. (This is particularly important to note with *L. pycnostachya*, *L. scariosa*, and their several cultivars.) A moderately fertile sandy soil and a position in full sun are about the only other requirements for *Liatris*. Division will be necessary sometime after the fourth year, depending upon growing conditions.

Stems of taller growing *L. pycnostachya*, *L. scariosa* 'September Glory', and *L.* 'White Spire' have a tendency to lean under their own weight and may require staking. For the gardener with stringent requirements for minimal maintenance, the lower-growing varieties would be best.

L. pycnostachya — Cat-tail or Kansas Gayfeather — Dense 5-foot spikes of purple or pinkish-lavender flowers in August and September. Stems well clothed with leaves.
Sources: 13,24,27,32,46,57,68; A,C,I,K,L

L. pycnostachya 'Alba' — White-flowered cultivar of the preceding species. 4 feet.
Sources: 67; K

L. scariosa — Tall Gayfeather — Purple flowers on 2 to 3-foot stems. Flowers in late August and September.
Sources: 4,24,57; I,K

L. scariosa 'September Glory' — Purple flowers which open almost simultaneously along the 5 to 6-foot stems. Late September.
Sources: 7,24,32,66,67,69; C,I,L

L. scariosa 'Snow White' — Pure white flowers on 4-foot stems in late August and September.
Sources: 24; I

L. scariosa 'White Spire' — A white-flowering sport of *L.* 'September Glory'.
Sources: 7,13,32,49,66,69; C

L. spicata — Spike Gayfeather — Bright purple flowers on 3-foot stems. Will tolerate wetter conditions than the other species.
Sources: 4,13,14,59,66,68; B,C,

Liatris spicata — *Spike Gayfeather. The flowers begin to open at the top of the spike.*

Liatris spicata — *Spike Gayfeather*

L. spicata 'Kobold' — Flowers dark purple, plants of compact growth habit.
Sources: 24,32,49,57,69; I,J,K,L

L. spicata 'Silver Tips' — Flowers lavender with a silvery sheen. 3 feet.
Source: 67

L. 'August Glory' — Deep bluish-purple flowers in August.
Source: 7

L. 'Orchid Pink' — Orchid-pink flowers on 5-foot spikes from mid-July into September.
Source: 7

Ligularia clivorum *'Desdemona'*

Ligularia clivorum 'Desdemona'
Var. of Bigleaf-Goldenray or Golden Groundsel
Daisy Family (Compositae)

Several species and cultivars of *Ligularia* could be used in our area, but this is the only one which seems available from nurseries at the present time. It is a bold, handsome plant with large purple tinged leaves up to 12 inches across; for these alone, the plant would be well worth growing. In mid- to late August, branched flower stalks 2½ to 3½ feet in height bearing numerous 2-inch orange-yellow flowers are produced. These last into early fall.

Plants are quite sensitive to drying out, and a good rich soil which contains ample organic matter should be provided. A position in partial shade is preferable to full sun where the large leaves are subject to wilting, especially after extended cloudy or rainy periods. They soon recover from this, however.

Large clumps up to 2½ feet wide are formed in fairly short order, so ample space should be provided at planting time; they can remain in place for years without requiring division. This plant often is found listed in catalogs under the genus name *Senecio*.

Sources: 13,24,68,69; C,I

Limonium   **Sea Lavender, Hardy Statice**
                                 Leadwort Family (Plumbaginaceae)

This is a small group of very long-lived plants for the herbaceous border.

Established plants bear numerous small flowers in large panicles. These are frequently up to 1½ feet across and can be used effectively in dried flower arrangements. In time, a clump may have up to a dozen flowering stems and form a spectacular canopy of flowers 2½ to 3 feet wide. Sea Lavender may be used in much the same way as *Gypsophila* (Baby's Breath) to impart a light, airy effect in the garden, and is an excellent substitute in areas where the latter does not overwinter well.

It is a fitting subject for gardens near the sea; inland, the major requirement is that plants be grown in a light sandy loam in a sunny position. If planted in a heavier soil, stems invariably will be weak and require staking. They may be supported by the hoop method discussed in the chapter on staking. The roots are very long, and will need large holes at planting time. Frequent division or transplanting is not advisable since it takes plants several years to become established and grow into sizeable specimens; they are best left entirely alone to improve as each year passes. *Limonium* is most frequently listed in catalogs under the old name *Statice*.

L. latifolium — Sea Lavender, Hardy Statice — The most important species for garden use. Bears masses of bright lavender flowers in July and August on stems up to 2½ feet in length. Full grown specimens may be up to a yard in width when in flower. The leathery green leaves are partially evergreen, and produced in rather small basal rosettes. For winter bouquets, cut the stems when the flowers are fully open and hang them upside down in a well ventilated, shady place.
Sources: 13,24,25,32,67,68,69; C,I,J,K

L. latifolium 'Colliers Pink' — An excellent pink-flowered form.
Source: 67

L. latifolium 'Violetta' — An excellent deep violet-blue flowered form.
Sources: 24,59,67; I

L. tataricum var. **angustifolium** (found in catalogs under the old name *L. dumosa*) — Lanceleaf Tatarian Sea Lavender — In no way is this superior to the preceding species, but it is worth growing for its large masses of silvery lavender flowers in August and September. Reaches a height of nearly 20 inches when in flower.
Sources: 24; I,J

Flax Family (Linaceae)

Although not dependably hardy much farther north than Boston, this is a group of otherwise long-lived plants which require little attention other than the occasional removal of self-sown seedlings.

A position in full sun with a light, well-drained soil is about all that is necessary. Soggy soil conditions in winter lessen the hardiness of the whole group.

The small flowers last only about a day, but they are borne in great profusion and appear over a long period of time. They are not useful when cut for bouquets.

L. *narbonense* — Narbonne Flax — 1-inch azure-blue flowers with white centers produced from late June through August. Plants 1½ to 2 feet in height.
Sources: 24,60; A,I

L. *narbonense* '**Heavenly Blue**' — Very heavy-flowering cultivar with deep blue blossoms on plants 12 to 18 inches in height.
Source: 69

L. *perenne* — Perennial Flax — Pale blue flowers, freely produced nearly all summer on 2-foot plants.
Sources: 3,14,46,66,68; B,J,K,L

L. *perenne* '**Album**' — White-flowered form of the preceding species.
Sources: 24,66; I

L. *perenne* '**Tetra Red**' — Satin red flowers on plants about 18 inches in height.
Sources: 24; I

The following may not be as robust or as long-lived as those which precede:

L. *alpinum* — Alpine Flax — This is probably better as a rock garden plant, but may occasionally have uses at the very front of the border. Slender plants with clear blue flowers in June on 6 to 9 inch stems. Narrow, almost Heather-like leaves.
Sources: 4,13,24; C,I

L. *flavum* — Golden Flax — Another species equally adapted to the rock garden or front of the border. The compact plants are about 15 to 18 inches in height with leathery leaves; bear numerous bright yellow waxy flowers from late June to mid-August.
Sources: 69; K

L. flavum 'Compactum' — A dwarf version of the preceding. Grows to a height of about 9 inches.
Sources: 3,4,24,60,68; I

Lobelia

Lobelia
Lobelia Family (Lobeliaceae)
It is a shame to have to condemn such a beautiful group of native plants, but under most garden situations they are short-lived perennials and will usually disappear after a few years. When they find conditions exactly to their liking, they will self-sow in quantity and always be around. For this reason it would be wise to experiment with a few plants to see if seeding will occur.

Lobelias are frequently associated with wet conditions because they are encountered in the wild along streams or in generally wet areas. In the garden, a well-drained, yet moisture-retentive loam is best. Light shade for at least part of the day is preferable, but a position in full sun will not be harmful if the soil is moist. Mulching the plants both in summer and winter is often beneficial when a permanent display is desired. When self-sowing does not occur, the new basal growth which appears in early fall after flowering may be divided and replanted. Seedlings sown in pans and set out annually also will provide a continuing display.

L. cardinalis — Cardinal Flower — Bright scarlet-red flowers on 3 to 4-foot stems from the end of July to early September distinguish this as one of the best-loved wild flowers of eastern North America.
Sources: 3,4,5,7,13,14,24,26,27,39,43,46,50,58,66,67,68; A,B,C,I, L

L. cardinalis 'Alba' — A rare white-flowered form of the Cardinal Flower. Does not reproduce true from seed and must be perpetuated by cuttings. Only worth growing by serious collectors of wild flowers.
Source: 29

L. siphilitica — Blue Cardinal Flower, Great Blue Lobelia — Not a very good name for a beautiful native plant. Has deep blue flowers and grows to 2 to 3 feet in height under garden conditions. The Indians believed that a concoction made from it was useful in curing venereal disease.
Sources: 4,7,26,27,39,43,57; B

L. × *vedariensis* (*L. cardinalis* × *L. siphilitica*) — A stunning hybrid with brilliant purple flowers from July well into September on spikes 2½ to 3 feet tall. Best results are obtained in the shade, and this plant definitely benefits from a protective mulch in the winter.
Sources: 4,13,66,69; C

Left: Lobelia cardinalis

[135]

Lupinus   **Lupine, Lupin**
                                              Pea Family (Leguminosae)
These cannot be recommended for general cultivation because of their sensitivity to hot summers. They do best in cool, humid areas such as northern New England and the Pacific Northwest. To those familiar with Lupines where they grow well, the show produced in our area is disappointing to say the very least. Of the several types which are hardy, the following strain is by far the showiest and most popular.

L. × *regalis* 'Russell Hybrids' — Stately spikes 3 to 4 feet in height with large pea-like flowers in nearly every color or combination imaginable.
Sources: 13,14,25,30,32,39,46,58,66,69; A,B,C,E,J,K,L

Lychnis   **Campion, Maltese Cross, German Catchfly**
                       Carnation Family (Caryophyllaceae)
Some members of this group of bright-flowered plants only can be recommended for a low maintenance situation if the soil is light, and very well drained. Others lack complete hardiness or are distressingly short-lived. All should be given a situation in full sun.

L. chalcedonica — Maltese Cross — Brilliant scarlet flowers in dense heads in June and July. Plants 2½ to 3 feet in height. Will be short-lived unless soil drainage is excellent, especially in winter.
Sources: 4,24,32,68; A,E,I,J,K,L

L. chalcedonica 'Alba' — The white flowers are not very interesting when compared to those of the species.
Sources: 24; I

L. viscaria — German Catchfly — This species and its several cultivars are the hardiest and longest-lived. The reddish-purple clustered blossoms appear on 12 to 18-inch stems in late May and June above tufts of grass-like foliage. If soil and exposure are correct, little care will be required other than division after about the fourth year.
Source: 46

L. viscaria 'Alba' — Short 9-inch spikes of white flowers in June and July.
Sources: 24; I

L. viscaria 'Splendens' — Bright rose-pink flowers.
Source: L

L. viscaria 'Splendens Flore-Pleno' — Double, bright rose-pink flowers.
Sources: 13,24,32,49,66,67,69; C,I,J,K

L. viscaria 'Zulu' — Flowers light red.
Sources: 32,66

> *L. coronaria* — Rose Campion, Mullein-pink — Short-lived, usually behaves as a biennial, but will seldom disappear from the garden as it seeds freely. Very bright, small reddish-purple flowers on 2-foot stems. Leaves silverish. Listed in some catalogs as *Agrostemma coronaria*.
> Sources: E,L

> *L.* × *haageana* (*L. fulgens* × *L. coronaria* var. *sieboldii*) — Haage Campion — Brilliantly colored flowers from orange-red to scarlet or salmon, produced from June to August. Plants about a foot in height. Hardiness sometimes questionable.
> Sources: 69; L

Lysimachia   Loosestrife
Primrose Family (Primulaceae)

Most members of this genus would not look well in a manicured, formal border because of the spreading tendency of the more commonly grown species; however, they are acceptable in the low maintenance situation if space permits.

Loosestrifes planted in full sun require soil that is moist and fairly rich. If the exposure is partial shade, much drier soil conditions are tolerated. Almost no care is needed if they are planted about 3 feet from their nearest neighbors; otherwise, an occasional reduction in the size of the clumps will become necessary. Division to rejuvenate the plants will not be required for a number of years.

L. clethroides — Gooseneck Loosestrife — The 3-foot densely-flowered spikes bend over at the tips producing the curious "gooseneck" appearance. Flowers are white; blooming time is July and August. Leaves turn a bronzy-yellow in the autumn. It bears repeating, with this species especially, that the clumps soon become large.
Sources: 13,49,66; C

L. punctata — Yellow Loosestrife — The leaves are produced in whorls around the stem, and the yellow flowers arise from these. Plants range in height from 2½ to 3 feet. Flowering time is June

and early July. Plants are at their best in light shade.
Sources: 14,24,32,66,67,69; I

> **L. nummularia** — Creeping Jenny, Moneywort — A low creeping plant not suited to the border. Best as a ground cover, used with discretion, in semishaded places. Will often escape into the lawn.
> Sources: 3,13,14,57; C

> **L. nummularia 'Aurea'** — Yellow-leaved cultivar of the preceding species.
> Sources: 24,68; I

Lysimachia clethroides

Lythrum   **Purple Loosestrife**
Loosestrife Family (Lythraceae)
The Purple Loosestrife, a native of Europe, is now so widely
naturalized that it is difficult to believe that it is only a comparatively recent addition to our flora.

A number of selections have been made. These vary considerably in height and flower color, many without the magenta
tint so conspicuous in the wild forms. They are worth culti-
vating, especially in difficult wet areas of the garden, and also
will grow perfectly well in an ordinary soil in full sun. Purple
Loosestrifes will tolerate almost any form of neglect and grow
vigorously for many years. They range in height, depending
upon cultivar, from 1½ to 4 feet and are suitable at the front
or middle of the border. They are best grown as single specimens, or in small groupings of two or three plants spaced 1½
to 2 feet apart. Most cultivars blossom over quite a long period
between June and the end of September.

L. salicaria — For garden situations, the species is not as interesting as the selections listed below, but it may find a place in
the wild flower garden or for naturalizing in wet places. It should
be remembered that this may seed freely and take over extensive
areas, frequently choking out all other vegetation. The named
cultivars do not seem to possess this tendency.
Sources: 4,7,14,39,45,66

L. salicaria 'Columbia' — Soft pink flowers on well-branched,
bushy plants about 3½ feet in height.
Sources: 28, 66; L

L. salicaria 'Dropmore Purple' — Rich violet-purple flowers on
plants 3 to 4 feet in height.
Sources: 13,24,69; C,I

L. salicaria 'Firecandle' — Intense rosy-red flowers. Plants 3 feet
in height.
Sources: 13,24; C,I

L. salicaria 'Happy' — Dark pink flowers on dwarf, well-branched plants, 15 to 18 inches in height.
Sources: 24,32,69; I

L. salicaria 'Morden's Gleam' — Flowers bright carmine, the
nearest to red of any of the cultivars. Plants 3 to 4 feet in height.
Sources: 13,28,32,37,39,59,69; C,H,J,K

Lythrum salicaria *Purple Spires*. Photo: P. Bruns.

L. salicaria 'Morden's Pink' — Flowers clear pink. Plants 3 to 4 feet in height.
Sources: 13,24,25,32,46,59,60,66,67,68; B,C,H,I,J,K,L

L. salicaria 'Morden's Rose' — Flowers bright rosy-red. Plants 3 feet in height.
Sources: 24,28; H,I

L. salicaria 'Pink Spires' — Bright pink flowers, plants 3½ to 4 feet in height.
Sources: 58; A

L. salicaria 'Purple Spires' — Rose-purple flowers, plants 3½ to 4 feet in height.
Sources: 28,32,37,58; A,H,K,L

L. salicaria 'Robert' — Flowers bright rose-red. Plants 2 feet in height. Very compact.
Sources: 3,14,24,30,37,59,68,69; B,H,I,J,K,L

L. salicaria 'The Beacon' — Flowers near-red. Plants 2½ feet in height.
Sources: 68; B

L. salicaria 'Tom's Choice' — Rosy-red flowers. Plants 3 to 3½ feet in height.
Source: 68

L. virgatum — Wand Loosestrife — Similar to *L. salicaria* with purple flowers on branched stems. Plants about 3 feet in height. The species is seldom offered by nurseries, but may have played a part in the parentage of a few of the cultivars listed above as *L. salicaria*. The following cultivar is of interest, primarily because of its low stature.

L. virgatum 'Rose Queen' — Rich rose-pink flowers on plants 2 feet in height.
Sources: 24; I

Macleaya cordata   **Plume-poppy, Tree-celandine**
                                        Poppy Family (Papaveraceae)
   This is almost universally listed in catalogs under the old name *Bocconia cordata*.
   Plume-poppy is a large plant that produces stems 6 to 8 feet tall with large scalloped leaves that are almost tropical in their effect. Under most conditions it tends to spread rapidly by its

wide ranging underground stems. It should not be considered for a small garden or a low maintenance situation.
Sources: 24,25,32,66,67,68,69; I,K

Mertensia virginica **Virginia Bluebell, Bluebell**
Borage Family (Boraginaceae)

This plant is indispensable to the spring garden, especially where true blue flowers are wanted. It grows to a height of about 2 feet with clusters of drooping, bell-like flowers in early May. The buds are soft pink and contrast nicely with the blue, opened flowers. A white-flowered form exists, but is very slow growing and not widely offered by nurseries.

This is not a plant for massing in the perennial border. After it blooms the foliage starts to die down and usually has disappeared by July. Therefore, *Mertensia* should be placed among plants with spreading summer foliage, such as Hostas or Ferns.

Plants will not require division for many years. For increase, this is best done in the early autumn, after the plants have died down. Cultivation in summer should be done with care around the dormant plants, and it would be prudent to mark their location in some way. They grow best in shady areas where the soil is cool and moist and contains ample organic matter.
Sources: 3,5,13,14,23,24,25,27,28,29,39,43,46,50,57,60,66,67, 68,69; B,C,I,L

Monarda didyma **Beebalm, Bergamot, Oswego Tea**
Mint Family (Labiatae)

In a strictly low maintenance situation, Beebalm may be recommended only for naturalizing in places where the plants can romp. In most herbaceous border situations, clumps spread rapidly, and division is necessary by the end of the second or third year to keep them in bounds and to prevent degeneration.

Plants grow to a height of 2½ to 3 feet and bloom from late June to August. The 2 to 3-inch tubular flowers are borne in single or double whorls forming dense heads, and are excellent for cutting purposes. The pungent, mint-like fragrance of the leaves and stems is another good feature.

Although Beebalms will tolerate light shade, such a condition encourages the spreading tendencies. A site offering full sun and soil with good moisture retention is best.

M. didyma — Flowers bright scarlet.
Sources: 14,27,39,46,68

Above and Below: Monarda didyma *'Violacea Superba'*

M. *didyma* 'Adam' — Ruby-red flowers. Probably the best of the red-flowered cultivars.
Sources: 13,24,29,30,66,67; C,I

M. *didyma* 'Blue Stocking' — Flowers bright violet-purple, not blue as the name would imply.
Source: 69

M. *didyma* 'Cambridge Scarlet' — Brilliant scarlet flowers.
Sources: 24,25,60,66,69; A,B,I,K,L

M. *didyma* 'Croftway Pink' — Rich rose-pink flowers.
Sources: 3,13,24,67,69; A,B,C,I,K,L

M. *didyma* 'Granite Pink' — Rose-pink flowers. More compact habit of growth than most of the other cultivars.
Sources: 29,66,68

M. *didyma* 'Mahogany' — Dark wine-red flowers.
Sources: 13,57,66,67,69; C

M. *didyma* 'Melissa' — Soft pink flowers.
Source: 69

M. *didyma* 'Prairie Brand' — Salmon-red flowers. Plants grow to a height of 4 feet, taller than most other cultivars.
Source: 69

M. *didyma* 'Salmonea' — Salmon-pink flowers.
Sources: 66,68

M. *didyma* 'Snow Queen' — White flowers.
Source: 69

M. *didyma* 'Snow White' — White flowers.
Sources: 24; I

M. *didyma* 'Violet Queen' — Lavender-violet flowers.
Sources: 13,24,66; C,I

Nepeta × *faassenii (N. mussinii* × *N. nepetella)*   Catmint
Mint Family (Labiatae)

This is listed invariably in nursery catalogs as *N. mussinii,* which is one of the parents.

N. × *faassenii* grows into a mound 15 to 18 inches wide and 10 to 12 inches in height, and is a valuable plant for the front of the border. Blue-violet flowers are produced abundantly on 12-inch stems from late May through July and intermittently thereafter until September. A heavy autumn flowering is produced if the stems are cut back to about half their length immediately after the first blooming finishes. This encourages vigorous new

growth from the base of the plant and helps to perpetuate a bushy habit. The small leaves are silvery-gray in color, a handsome contrast to the blue flowers. They give an unpleasant pungent aroma when bruised.
Sources: 3,13,24,45,66,67,68,69; C,E,I,L

N. × **faassenii 'Blue Wonder'** — Lavender-blue flowers on compact, 12 to 15-inch mounds.
Sources: J,K

> **N. cataria** — Catnip — Easy to grow and beloved by cats and bees, but too nondescript to find a home in a real perennial garden. Besides the few sources listed here, the plant is readily found in the catalogs of the various herb specialists.
> Sources: 45,68
>
> **N. 'Six Hills Giant'** — A beautiful light blue-flowered hybrid with gray leaves that grows to a height of about 2 feet. It is rampant and spreading and would soon become an untidy nuisance in a low maintenance situation.
> Source: 66

Oenothera   **Evening Primrose, Sundrops**
                          Evening Primrose Family (Onagraceae)
Plants of this group that open their flowers during the day are called Sundrops; those that are night bloomers are Evening Primroses.

O. missouriensis — Ozark Sundrop — Here is an American plant that may be grown in any garden offering a well-drained light soil, and space in the sun. If these conditions can be provided, plants will thrive for many years and make few other demands.

Ozark Sundrop is a low plant with a somewhat sprawling habit, not over 8 inches in height, and useful at the front of the border. The 5-inch, golden-yellow, cup-like flowers are quite spectacular. They appear over a long period of time from June through August and have a mild fragrance. The plant is late to appear in the spring so its location should be marked.
Sources: 14,24,25,27,49,59,66,67,68,69; A,I,J,K,L

> **O. tetragona** — Common Sundrop — This is listed in catalogs under the following names: *O. fruticosa* var. *youngii, O. youngii.* The species is quite hardy. It is very showy in flower and may be grown where minimal maintenance is not the aim. Soil conditions and exposure are the same as required by *O. missouri-*

[145]

ensis. Plants grow to a height of about 2 feet. The lemon-yellow, 1½-inch, cup-shaped flowers are borne in profusion throughout June and July.
Sources: 29,46,66,67,69; L,B,K

O. tetragona 'Highlight' — Large yellow flowers on plants 18 inches in height.
Sources: 24; I

O. tetragona 'Yellow River' — The standard variety. Large canary-yellow flowers up to 2 inches across on plants about 1½ feet in height.
Sources: 3,13,24,68; C,I

O. tetragona var. *fraseri* 'Illumination' (may be listed as *O. fyrverkeri*, or *O.* 'Fireworks') — Deep yellow flowers on plants 15 inches in height with leathery bronze foliage; the young stems and flower buds are reddish-brown. A good plant for rock gardens.
Sources: 24,32; I

Below: Partially open blossom of Oenothera missouriensis.
Photo: P. Bruns.

Paeonia   **Peony, Paeony**
                              Peony Family (Paeoniaceae)

Peonies are most fitting perennials for the low maintenance garden. The relative ease of culture combined with an exceedingly long life, great hardiness, and their popularity as cut flowers make them nearly indispensable.

Plants that are to last thirty years and sometimes more in one spot require a deep, rich, well-drained soil. Plenty of humus should be incorporated at planting time, but manure, especially fresh manure, should never come in contact with the thick, fleshy root system. Divisions should contain at least three to five buds or eyes at the top of the roots, and these should be set about 1 inch below the soil line. Deeper planting leads to poor flowering, or no flowers at all. Late August or early September is the preferred time for planting or transplanting. Although a site in full sun is the usual recommendation, the more delicately colored varieties can be placed in light shade to keep the flowers from fading quickly. Deep shade should be avoided. This produces the same result as planting too deeply: few flowers, or none at all. Blossoms also may be lost if buds are nipped by late spring frost.

Larger flowers can be produced if the lateral flower buds are removed early, taking care not to injure the terminal bud. This usually will be done only by the perfectionist, even though it takes but a few moments.

Peony flowers come in a number of types as well as colors. The Doubles last longest, the stamens and sometimes the carpels being petal-like so that a fully double flower results. The Singles (sometimes called Chinese type) have one or several rows of petals that surround a center of numerous yellow stamens. This simpler type may be preferred by those who find the Doubles too flamboyant. The Japanese type and the Anemone type are often lumped together in catalogs. The former have five or more quite large petals that surround a center of stamens bearing abortive anthers (the part that normally contains pollen). The filaments (the "stemlike" part of the stamen) are thick and enlarged. In the Anemone type the filaments have become narrow, incurved petal-like structures.

So many cultivars are available from specialist nurserymen that only a few of the better ones can be included here. Each year sees the advent of new ones, and gardeners interested in the group would do well to join the American Peony Society.

[147]

Double types:

P. 'Albert Crousse' — Soft pink. Fairly late flowering.
Sources: 68; H

P. 'Festiva Maxima' — White. Early flowering.
Sources: 3,8,12,13,20,23,24,30,37,59,60,65,66,68,69; C,H,I,M

P. 'Karl Rosenfeld' — Dark red. Midseason flowering.
Sources: 6,8,12,20,24,37,59,66,68,69; H,I,M

P. 'LeCygne' — White. Early midseason flowering.
Sources: 13,66,67,68; C,H,M

P. 'Lowell Thomas' — Brassy red, crinkled petals, dwarf. Midseason flowering.
Sources: 6,31,69

Single types:

P. 'Clair de Lune' — Yellow. Very early flowering.
Sources: 44,65,68

P. 'Pico' — White. Midseason flowering.
Sources: 6,40,66

Above: Paeonia lactiflora *cultivar.*

Left: Foliage of herbaceous peonies remains attractive throughout the growing season.

Japanese and anemone types:

P. 'Alstead' — Deep pink with yellow center.
Sources: 8; M

P. 'Ama-no-sode' — Bright pink with yellow center.
Sources: 8,40,65,68,69

P. 'Mikado' — Bright red, rose stamens tipped with gold. Mid-season flowering.
Sources: 13,24,68; C,H,I,M

P. 'Nippon Brilliant' — Bright red.
Sources: 8,65,66

Papaver orientale   **Poppy, Oriental Poppy**
                                          Poppy Family (Papaveraceae)
Oriental Poppies now can be obtained in such a beautiful array of colors that it is unfortunate many people still associate this group only with the orange-scarlet types. Cultivars with showy flowers 6 to 12 inches across that range in color from white to pink, red and near yellow, deserve consideration today. Of these, the white varieties probably should be avoided as they tend to be rather short-lived, and the flowers often become gray from their own pollen. The so-called yellows are basically orange with a yellow tinge.

Oriental poppies are bold plants, 2 to 4 feet in height when in flower, with coarse, hairy lobed leaves. In time clumps become large: up to a yard across in some varieties. In small gardens, one or two plants are all that will be necessary.

About their only fault in a low maintenance situation is the tendency of the stems of some of the more vigorous cultivars to flop under the weight of the flowers. This can be remedied easily (see staking methods, page 203).

A well-drained soil of moderate fertility, and full sun or partial shade are required. Wet soil conditions in winter lead to a rapid demise. The flowering season is relatively short and the plants disappear entirely from July to September; conspicuous gaps in the garden will result if they have been massed. The leaves reappear in the autumn and remain throughout the winter. Plants can be divided or transplanted only in August or September and generally do not bloom until the second year after transplanting. It is prudent to provide a mulch for the first winter.

Papaver orientale *cultivar*

Poppies may be used as cut flowers if the ends of the stems are seared with a flame before being placed in water.

Over sixty named cultivars are presently available from nurseries. The following selection illustrates the marvelous color range.

P. orientale **'Barr's White'** — Large pure white flowers with purplish-black markings at the base of the petals.
Sources: 3,13,24,66,67; C,I

P. orientale **'Beauty of Livermore'** — Deep red flowers with black spots at the base of the petals.
Sources: 23,68; A,K,L

P. orientale **'Bonfire'** — Bright orange-red flowers with crinkly-edged petals.
Sources: 12,54,66,67

P. orientale **'Burgundy'** — Maroon-red flowers.
Sources: 13,24,66,68; C,I

P. orientale **'Carnival'** — Flowers vivid orange-red, white at the lower half of each petal.
Sources: 12,13,24,28,32,37,60; C,I

P. orientale **'Crimson Pompom'** — Fully double deep red flowers.
Sources: 13,24,60; C,I

P. orientale **'Curtis Mahogany'** — Very dark maroon-red flowers with crinkled petals like crepe paper.
Sources: 32,59

P. orientale **'Dubloon'** — Fully double clear orange flowers.
Sources: 13,24,66; C,I

P. orientale **'Field Marshal Von der Glotz'** — Large white flowers with black markings at the base of the petals.
Sources: 13,24,28,32,37,59; C,I

P. orientale **'Glowing Embers'** — Crimson-red flowers.
Sources: 13,24,66; C,I,L

P. orientale **'Glowing Rose'** — Large luminous watermelon-pink flowers.
Sources: 12,24,32; I

P. orientale **'Harvest Moon'** — Clear golden-orange flowers.
Sources: 3,13,24,28,59,60,66,68; C,I

P. orientale 'Helen Elizabeth' — Light pink flowers with dark markings at the base of the petals.
Sources: 3,12,13,24,28,32,59,66,67,68; C,I

P. orientale 'Henry Cayeux Imp' — Flowers smoky-rose with lavender tints.
Sources: 24,37; I

P. orientale 'Lavender Glory' — Deep lavender flowers with large black spots at the base of the petals.
Sources: 13,24,59,60,66; C,I

P. orientale 'May Curtis' — Watermelon-red flowers.
Sources: 13,24,28,68; C,I

P. orientale 'Mrs. Perry' — Flowers salmon-pink with an apricot tinge.
Sources: 13,24,60; C,I,L

P. orientale 'Pinnacle' — Flowers white with flame colored edges.
Sources: 3,13,24,66,67; C,I

P. orientale 'Queen Alexandria' — Bright salmon-pink flowers.
Sources: 3; A,K,L

P. orientale 'Raspberry Queen' — Raspberry colored flowers.
Sources: 28,32,66

P. orientale 'Salome' — Clear rose-pink flowers.
Sources: 3,13,24,32,37,59,67,68; C,I

P. orientale 'Surprise' — Large vermillion-red flowers.
Sources: 12,13,24,67; C,I

P. orientale 'Warlord' — Probably the finest deep crimson-red cultivar.
Sources: 3,13,24,59,66,68; C,I,L

Papaver nudicaule cultivars — Iceland Poppy — These have strong tendencies to behave as biennials in our area and are frequently treated as annuals. Under suitable conditions they often self-sow freely, but the several fine cultivars available may not reproduce themselves true to variety.

Phlox paniculata (syn. *P. decussata*) **Summer Phlox, Garden Phlox**
Polemonium Family (Polemoniaceae)
Susceptibility to mildew, rust, and red spider attacks, combined with the need for thinning new growth annually and dividing about every third year, should be sufficient reasons to ban

[153]

this handsome group from the low maintenance garden. Also, they require frequent watering during the growing season, and self-sow easily, producing plants of inferior color. For those who are prepared to spray every two weeks against the diseases and pests, few other plants are as showy as Summer Phloxes over such a long period of time in the border. For those who cannot take the time, few other plants will produce such a ragged, tattered appearance.

Summer Phloxes require a deep, rich soil, and full sun or light shade. Thorough deep irrigation in dry periods during the growing season is necessary. Cultivars range in height from 2 to 4 feet and bloom from late June into September. Removal of the faded flower heads prolongs the blossoming period. Flowers range in color from pink in all its shades to red, pale blue to purple, and white. Catalogs often list a group called Symons-Jeune Phlox, which are the celebrated cultivars produced in England by the late Captain B. Symons-Jeune, one of the most noted breeders of Summer Phlox.

P. paniculata 'Blue Ice' — Pinkish-blue at the center when they first open, the flowers turn white as they age.
Sources: 7,24,69; I

P. paniculata 'Dodo Hanbury Forbes' — One of the best with clear pink flowers. Huge pyramidal flower heads up to 14 or 16 inches across.
Sources: 1,7,13,20,24,32,60,66,67,69; B,C,G,I,J,K,L

P. paniculata 'Dresden China' — Flowers soft shell-pink with a deeper "eye" at the center.
Sources: 7,13,23,24,59,67,68,69; C,G,I,J,K,L

P. paniculata 'Fairy's Petticoat' — Very large light pink flowers with a darker pink "eye" at the center. Very long period of flowering.
Sources: 7,24,44,60,66,67,68,69; H,I,J,K,L

P. paniculata 'Juliet' — Pale pink flowers. Plants 2 feet in height.
Sources: 24,69; I

P. paniculata 'Lilac Time' — Lilac-blue flowers.
Sources: 7,13,24,32,37,67; C,H,I,J

P. paniculata 'Mount Fujiyama' — Pure white flowers.
Sources: 13,24,28,67,68; B,C,I

P. paniculata 'Orange Perfection' — Near-orange flowers.
Sources: 3,13,66,67; C,L

P. paniculata 'Pinafore Pink' — Probably the lowest growing cultivar. Plants about 6 inches in height. Flowers bright pink with a deeper pink "eye" at the center.
Sources: 24,66,67; L

P. paniculata 'Rembrandt' — Pure white flowers.
Sources: 59,68,69

P. paniculata 'Russian Violet' — Bright violet-purple flowers.
Sources: 15,20,24,60,66,67; I,J,L

P. paniculata 'Sir John Falstaff' — Very large, luminous salmon-pink flowers with a darker "eye" at the center.
Sources: 3,13,23,24,32,44,46,59,66,69; B,C,I,K,L

P. paniculata 'Starfire' — Brilliant deep red flowers.
Sources: 1,3,13,15,20,24,25,28,30,32,37,44,58,59,60,66,67,69; B, C,G,H,I,J,K,L

P. paniculata 'White Admiral' — Very large clusters of white flowers.
Sources: 3,13,15,20,23,24,37,58,60,66,67,68,69; B,C,G,H,I,J,K,L

P. paniculata 'World Peace' — Pure white flowers in September.
Sources: 24,32,59,66,69; I,J,L

Below: Powdery mildew on the leaves of Phlox paniculata.

Although the following species of *Phlox* with their numerous varieties and cultivars are frequently listed in catalogs dealing with perennials, they are best either in the rock garden or the wild flower garden. Under most conditions they would not fit into the flower border because of their low stature and spreading habit: P. *divaricata* (Spring Phlox), P. *nivalis* (Trailing Phlox), P. *stolonifera* (Creeping Phlox), and P. *subulata* (Moss Pink, Ground Pink).

Physostegia	False Dragonhead, Obedient Plant, Stay-in-Place
	Mint Family (Labiatae)

One could almost forgive this group for its invasive tendencies were it not for the fact that the plants also require annual or biennial division to maintain any semblance of neatness. As they grow with relative indifference to wet or dry conditions and will tolerate sun or partial shade, they are of value for naturalizing in a semiwild area or an informal wild flower garden. But they should be used in herbaceous borders only when time can be devoted to keeping them in bounds.

The common names for *Physostegia* are of some interest. False Dragonhead refers to the one-time confusion between this genus and *Dracocephalum* (Dragonhead). Obedient Plant, or Stay-in-Place, refers to the fact that the individual flowers can be twisted on the stem and will remain as they are arranged, a characteristic that fascinates children.

P. *virginiana* — Grows to a height of 3 to 3½ feet and produces spikes of purplish-red flowers from July to September. The named cultivars are of much greater value than the species.
Sources: 4,14,27,39,43

P. *virginiana* var. *alba* — Flowers pure white on spikes about 1½ to 2 feet in height.
Sources: 30,69; K

P. *virginiana* 'Bouquet Rose' — Flowers rose-pink on spikes 3 feet in height.
Sources: 24,66,69; I,K

P. *virginiana* 'Rosy Spire' — Later in flowering than the other cultivars. Rose-pink flowers in early September on plants 3 to 3½ feet tall.
Sources: 39,66,68

P. *virginiana* 'Summer Glow' — Rosy crimson flowers on 3-foot plants.
Source: 32

P. *virginiana* 'Summer Snow' — White flowers on 2½-foot spikes. Less invasive than the other varieties, but requires the same frequent division.
Sources: 13,14,24,32,66,67,68; B,C,I

Physostegia virginiana *var.* alba

P. virginiana 'Variegata' — Deep green and white variegated leaves. Flowers pink.
Sources: 24,32,66; I

P. virginiana 'Vivid' — The lowest growing and most compact cultivar, but just as invasive as the rest. Glowing deep rosy pink flowers in early September on plants 2 feet in height.
Sources: 13,24,66,67; B,C,I,L

Platycodon   Balloon Flower
                                  Bellflower Family (Campanulaceae)

P. grandiflorum is the only species, but there are a few varieties and several cultivars that are easily grown and live for many years in a single place.

The roots of Balloon Flowers are thick and fleshy and cannot tolerate wet ground. A light, well-drained soil of moderate fertility suits them best. The pink varieties may fade unless planted in partial shade, but full sun is best for the blue-flowered or white-flowered types. New plants are rather slow of growth, but established clumps may be expected to thrive for twenty years and longer if they are not disturbed. They have no spreading tendencies, no major insect or disease problems, and they blossom from late June through July. Most varieties grow to a height of 3 feet and in some situations there may be a tendency for the stems to flop. This is easily remedied by supporting them by the hoop method described on page 203. Growth is late to start in spring, so early cultivation around the plants must be done with care. Balloon Flowers are seen to best advantage in groups of three spaced about 15 inches apart near the middle of the border. The flowers may be used for cutting purposes if the ends of the stems are seared with a flame before being placed in water.

P. grandiflorum — Chinese Balloon Flower — Handsome 2 to 3-inch cup-like blue flowers with prominent veins borne on stems 2 to 3 feet in height.
Sources: 3,13,14,23,46,67,69; B,C,J,L

P. grandiflorum var. album — White-flowered form.
Sources: 3,13,24,46,66,67,68,69; B,C,I,J,K,L

P. grandiflorum 'Apoyama' — A choice dwarf cultivar only 6 to 10 inches high from Japan. Highly prized on the rock garden, it has novelty value at the front of the border as well. Violet-

Platycodon grandiflorum *var.* mariesii

blue flowers almost all summer.
Source: 32

P. grandiflorum var. *mariesii* — Marie's Balloon Flower — One of the most compact forms, about 18 inches in height. Stems do not have the tendency to flop. Bright blue flowers.
Sources: 14,24,46,66,67,68; B,I,K,L

P. grandiflorum var. *mariesii album* — White-flowered form.
Source: 68

P. grandiflorum 'Shell Pink' — Soft shell-pink flowers veined deeper pink on plants 18 to 24 inches in height. Might be best planted in semishade.
Sources: 13,24,25,69; C,I,J,K,L

Plumbago larpentae — See *Ceratostigma plumbaginoides*

Polemonium   **Jacob's Ladder**
Polemonium Family (Polemoniaceae)
For refined, delicately textured foliage effects, this small group of mound-like plants is of value in the garden, even though the flowers will never set the world afire with their brilliance. Nonetheless, the terminal clusters of small cup-shaped pale to medium blue flowers appear in spring and early summer at a time when blue in the garden is particularly welcome.

Relatively undemanding, these are plants for light or partial shade. They require soil of at least average fertility with good drainage. Hot sunny places where the plants will bake are definitely unsuitable; in such situations the foliage becomes unsightly by midsummer.

P. caeruleum — Jacob's Ladder — Some common names are self-explanatory, others such as this really stretch the imagination. This plant's leaves, composed of numerous opposite leaflets, supposedly resemble the ladder in Jacob's dream.

The clear blue flowers are borne in nodding panicles at the top of erect, 15-inch stems during the month of May.
Source: 14

P. caeruleum var. lacteum (syn. *P. caeruleum* 'Album,' by which it is listed in catalogs). White-flowered form.
Source: 69

P. caeruleum 'Blue Pearl' — Cobalt-blue flowers with yellow centers or "eyes."
Sources: 3,13,14,24,59,66,67,68,69; C,I

P. reptans — Creeping Jacob's Ladder — Again, the common name may be misleading. The plants do not creep; they sprawl, and produce mounds up to 2 feet in width. Flowers are light blue with white centers or "eyes." These appear from May through June.
Sources: 27,43,66

[160]

Right: Polemonium reptans. *Photo: P. Bruns.*

Polygonatum   Solomon's Seal
                                          Lily Family (Liliaceae)
A small group of plants, handsome in leaf, long-lived, and of
special use in shady parts of the border in rich moist soil. The
white flowers appear in late May or June, hanging on short
stalks from the axils of the erect opposite leaves. It is for the
handsome foliage effect of deep green leaves on arching stems
up to 3 to 4 feet in height that the plants are mainly grown.
There are no insect or disease problems. Specimens seldom, if
ever, require division, but this may be done in early spring for
increase.

P. biflorum — Small Solomon's Seal — Grows to heights of 1½
to 3 feet, depending upon soil conditions. The flowers are borne
either singly, or more often in groups of two at each leaf axil.
Sources: 7,14,26,39,43,57,66; B

P. commutatum — True Solomon's Seal, Great Solomon's Seal —
The tallest and probably the most handsome species in general
cultivation. With good soil conditions plants often attain a
height of 3½ to 4 feet.
Sources: 1,7,14,26,39,66

P. multiflorum — Solomon's Seal, Lady's Seal, David's Harp — This is a European and Northern Asian counterpart to our native *P. biflorum* and *P. commutatum.* It reaches a maximum height of 3 feet.
Sources: 59,66,69; C

| *Primula* | Primrose |

Primrose Family (Primulaceae)

This genus, containing hundreds of species varying from minute alpines to 4-foot bog lovers, is so diverse that it has been divided into some 30 sections according to botanical detail (flower structure) and cultural requirements. All except two are native to cool moist areas throughout the Northern hemisphere and most do not adapt readily to the cold winters and hot summers of the Northeastern United States. Soil and moisture demands vary with the section, but all need high shade, a summer mulch, and deep watering during dry periods. A winter covering also should be provided in areas of uncertain snow cover.

The following descriptions are limited to a few species and cultivars that are suitable for the perennial garden, and easy to obtain and maintain.

P. auricula — Auricula — One of a group of hardy European alpines with rosettes of leathery evergreen leaves. All these need rock garden conditions, but the hybrid forms of *P. auricula* are larger and less demanding and can be grown in very well-drained fertile soil with a stone chip mulch to protect the crowns and woody stems from excess moisture.

The umbels of fragrant flowers on 6 to 8-inch stems have a white "eye" and a wide range of unusual muted colors. The whole plant is often powdered with white meal or farina.
Sources: 14,50,67; G

P. auricula 'Lynn Hall Strain' — A fine mixture of seedlings containing the full range of colors.
Sources: 32,44,49

P. auricula 'Monarch Strain' — Another mixture containing the full color range. Leaves silvery.
Sources: C,I

P. denticulata — Himalayan Primrose — This species has unique round flower heads up to 2 inches across, containing numerous small lilac flowers that open among the expanding leaves in April. In the autumn it forms a large dormant bud that sits on the soil surface throughout the winter. *P. denticulata* needs some protection and perfect drainage; it could be tried in conditions similar to those mentioned for *P. auricula.*
Sources: 4,32,43,49,66,69; B

P. denticulata var. *alba* — White-flowered form.
Sources: 29,69

Primula japonica — Japanese Primrose — In deep rich soil this species will thrive and spread by self-sown seed without the waterside conditions it prefers; but it must have summer irrigation and constant shade. Since the plants can be left for a number of years without disturbance, a generous mulch of manure or compost applied before leaves appear in the spring will help maintain soil fertility. In late autumn after the plants have become dormant a 4-inch mulch of hay or pine needles is a precaution against winter heaving.

In late May the first tier of flowers opens just above the leaves, and successive tiers appear for several weeks on the stems that may reach a height of 3 feet. Flower color is typically magenta, but includes white, and shades of pink and crimson.
Sources: 4,32,43,49,66,67,68

Primula × polyantha — Polyanthus Primrose — The result of crossing P. vulgaris veris and P. elatior, P. × polyantha has been the subject of much hybridization and is now available in a bewildering array of colors and forms. Although this is probably the most universally grown of primroses, it requires more frequent division and heavier feeding than some of the species to maintain the size and quantity of the often enormous flowers; it also is more subject to infestation of red spider. Some of the cultivars are not completely hardy.

P. × polyantha — Mixed colors — unnamed varieties.
Sources: 3,14,43,46,49,58,66; L

P. × polyantha — Separate colors — unnamed varieties.
Sources: 69; C,L

P. × polyantha 'Colossea Hybrids' — Large-flowered hybrids in shades of yellow, pink, copper, and red. (Sometimes listed in catalogs as P. veris 'Colossea Hybrids'.)
Sources: 24,32,68; B,I,J

P. × polyantha 'Pacific Giants' — Very free-flowering strain with large flowers and an extensive color range.
Sources: 24,32,44,53,60,67,68; G,I,K,L

P. sieboldii — Siebold Primrose — This species is distinguished by its crinkly and scalloped deciduous leaves. It appears very late in the spring, and if conditions are dry, may disappear soon after flowering, leaving at the surface a mat of rhizomes. This is very easy to divide for increase and should be marked against careless cultivation. The flowers appear in late May or early June and are borne in umbels on 10 to 12-inch stems. They range in color from white to shades of pink and rose.
Sources: 4,32,66

P. vulgaris — Common Primrose — More often listed in catalogs as P. acaulis, this is the fragrant early primrose of English hedgerow fame. It is an early-flowering evergreen species that is easy to grow in rich humus soil in woodland conditions; to maintain vigor, however, the plants should be divided and replanted in fresh soil every three or four years. A light winter covering of oak leaves or pine boughs will protect the leaves during open winters.

Flowers of the various cultivars come in white and shades of yellow, blue, purple, orange, and red. They are fragrant, appear very early in the spring, and are excellent for cutting.

The following list *P. vulgaris* in a mixture of colors.
Sources: 14,22,24,66; C,I,L

The following list *P. vulgaris* cultivars in the sought-after shade of blue.
Sources: 22,67

Individual named cultivars are listed by the following (Number 22 has a particularly comprehensive list).
Sources: 22,24; I

Pulmonaria   Lungwort
Borage Family (Boraginaceae)

This is a small group with only a few varieties, but it provides us with plants of low stature, early flowers, and foliage that remains attractive from spring to autumn. Plants are effective as single specimens, but are used more frequently in groups, spaced about 10 inches apart to give a ground cover effect. The drooping clusters of trumpet-shaped ½-inch flowers appear late in April and May on stems about a foot in height. They often open pink, then change to clear blue. Some varieties have clear pink or white flowers that do not undergo a change in color as they age. Any shady position where the soil is moist and cool, but not necessarily rich, seems to suit them.

Although it is frequently stated that the Lungworts should be divided every four years, they often last in good condition for much longer periods, and division is only necessary when plants have become overcrowded. Because they commence growth early in spring, late summer is the most convenient time to divide the plants. When this is done, frequent watering is necessary to encourage the development of a good root system before the onset of cold weather.

P. angustifolia — Blue or Cowslip Lungwort, Mary and Joseph, Soldiers-and-Sailors — Flowers open pink and turn to blue or deep blue. The deeper blue forms receive names in catalogs such as 'Azurea' or 'Coerulea.' The hairy green leaves are not spotted with white as are those of *P. saccharata*.
Sources: 3,32,66,67,68,69

[164]

Right: Pulmonaria saccharata. The distinctive spots on the leaves make Bethlehem Sage particularly valuable as a foliage plant.

P. saccharata — Bethlehem Sage — Even if this did not flower at all, it still would be valuable in the garden. The handsome 3 to 6-inch deep green leaves have numerous white spots that help to create a distinctive appearance. Flowers are bluish or reddish-violet.
Sources: 14,68

P. saccharata 'Mrs. Moon' — Large pink buds and showy deep blue flowers.
Sources: 3,32,66,67

P. saccharata 'Pink Dawn' — Bright rose-pink flowers.
Source: 69

Rudbeckia — Cone Flower
Daisy Family (Compositae)

The cultivars listed in catalogs under the name of *R. purpurea* are to be found in this discussion under *Echinacea purpurea*. The garden varieties in the genus *Rudbeckia* have yellow flowers, often with a dark "cone" or center, and resemble our native Black-eyed Susans. Those belonging to the genus *Echinacea*

have Daisy-like flowers in colors ranging from pink to red or white.

Rudbeckia is a genus of mixed blessings for the low maintenance gardener. Selections of R. hirta called the Gloriosa Daisies have handsome, large single or double flowers all summer long in shades of yellow to orange or mahogany. They are more apt to captivate the gardener than any other Rudbeckia, and are sometimes advertised as "perennials"; on all but the best-drained soils they invariably behave as annuals.

Another of the group, R. laciniata var. hortensis, is commonly known as "Golden Glow." It is a true perennial, towering to 7 feet in height. It produces 2 to 3-inch double yellow flowers for most of the summer; these are excellent for cutting purposes. A cultivar of this species, R. 'Gold Quelle,' discussed below, does not romp and is much better suited to a low maintenance situation.

For the few Cone Flowers that can be recommended, culture is quite simple. They must have full sun and soil of average fertility; good winter drainage is essential. All the cultivars listed here probably will require division for rejuvenation after the fourth or fifth year. Plant them in groups of three or more spaced about 12 inches apart at the middle of the border. All are excellent as cut flowers.

R. nitida 'Autumn Sun' (the correct cultivar name is 'Herbstsonne' but it is listed by its English translation in American catalogs) — Grows to a height of 4 to 5 feet and produces 3 to 4-inch, Black-eyed Susan-type flowers. The stems are rugged and staking is not required. Flowers through July and August.
Sources: 13; C

R. laciniata 'Golde Quelle' — Plants reach a height of only 2½ feet and clumps increase very slowly. The bright, double yellow flowers appear in profusion from July to September.
Sources: 14,24,32,66; I

R. fulgida var. sullivantii 'Goldsturm' — This is probably the finest cultivar in the genus, and represents the Black-eyed Susan to perfection. The deep yellow flowers with near-black "cones" or centers are 3 to 4 inches across and are freely produced on well-branched 2½ foot plants. They start to appear in mid-July and continue through September. Although this cultivar does not perform well in dry soil, it is one of the best perennials for continuous summer color in a low maintenance situation.
Sources: 13,14,24,32,59,60,66,67,69; C,B,I

[166]

Salvia   Salvia, Sage
                                              Mint Family (Labiatae)

A number of the Salvias are quite hardy in this area, but certainly not in every location or in every garden. Some people can grow them well, and others have fleeting success. A few species are biennial or otherwise short-lived and must be raised from seed every few years. The well-known red-flowering types are tropical perennials that are treated as annuals.

All perennial Sages require full sun and well-drained soil. Too much moisture at the roots in winter causes certain death, and most species should have the protection of a winter mulch. They often tolerate positions where they bake in summer, and will withstand a surprising amount of drought.

S. azurea — Azure Salvia — Native to the Southeast, it can be grown as far north as Vermont but is not reliably hardy without a good snow cover in the winter. Whorls of icy blue flowers on 4 to 5-foot stems in August and September.
Sources: 57,66

S. azurea var. *grandiflora* (syn. *S. pitcheri*, the name by which it is frequently listed in catalogs) — Pitcher's Salvia — Deep blue flowers. Plants 3 to 3½ feet in height.
Sources: 13,24,67,68; C,I

S. glutinosa — Sticky Salvia — The large flowers are pale yellow. Plants 3 feet in height. Somewhat coarse in appearance. Blooms in July.
Sources: 24; I

S. haematodes — One of the most conspicuous species when in blossom. Flowers are lavender-blue in large panicles during June. Plants are about 3 feet in height. Often behaves as a biennial.
Sources: 67,69

S. jurisicii — This species is perfectly hardy in our area, but its 8-inch height and habit of growth better fit the plant to the rock garden. Perhaps of some use at the very front of the border as edging. Forms mat-like clumps and produces violet-blue flowers for most of the summer if seed production is prevented.
Sources: 4,69

S. sclarea 'Vatican Variety' — Has strong biennial tendencies. Large silvery leaves with a somewhat unpleasant odor. Lavender-pink and white flowers on 3-foot stalks.
Source: 67

S. sclarea $\times$ *superba* 'May Night' — Violet-blue flowers from May to August if seed formation is prevented. Plants 1½ to 2 feet in height.
Sources: 28,69

Salvia $\times$ *superba* (frequently found in catalogs as *S. nemorosa*) — If seed production is prevented, this and its cultivars will flower from mid-June until late August. The flowers are violet or purple with reddish-purple calyces. Plants are about 2½ to 3 feet in height and quite hardy.
Sources: 68; B,J,L

S. $\times$ *superba* 'East Friesland' (listed in some catalogs as 'Ostfriesland') — Much branched 18-inch plants with violet-blue flowers in erect spikes.
Sources: 3,66,67,69; I,J

Scabiosa   **Pincushion Flower, Mourning Bride**
                              Teasel Family (Dipsacaceae)
  Here is another good group for the low maintenance gardener who can provide a sunny spot and a sandy loam enriched with compost.

The "flowers" are really an inflorescence, similar to Sunflowers. Their globular shape with the stamens sticking out of the individual florets has earned them the name "Pincushion."

Varieties recommended here grow to a height of 2 to 2½ feet and have flowers in shades of blue to white. They are excellent for cutting and are long lasting. The flowering season spans the months of June to September.

After the fourth year clumps may become crowded and need dividing for rejuvenation. This is best done in the early spring using only the young divisions growing vigorously from the outer portions of the old clumps. Scabiosas have no serious pests or diseases, and staking will not be required; they are most effective planted in groups of at least three, spaced 12 to 15 inches apart near the front or middle of the border.

S. caucasica — Caucasian Scabiosa — This species and its several cultivars are the only Scabiosas recommended for the flower border; the others are best in a rock garden situation. *S. caucasica* has 3-inch blue flowers with contrasting gray stamens.
Sources: 3,14,59,66,67; L

S. caucasica var. *alba* — White-flowered form.
Sources: 13,67; C,K

S. caucasica 'Blue Snowflake' — Rich amethyst-blue flowers.
Sources: 29,32

S. caucasica 'Constancy' — Amethyst-blue flowers.
Source: 32

S. caucasica 'Isaac House Hybrids' (sometimes also listed in catalogs as "House Mixture" or "House Hybrids") — The somewhat unusual name refers to their place of origin at Isaac House, Bristol, England. They are a mixture of shades that are basically lavender-blue.
Sources: 13,68; A,C,J,K

S. caucasica 'Miss Wilmott' — Pure white flowers.
Source: 32

S. alpina — Alpine Scabiosa — Typical small mauve-blue "pincushion" flowers on tufty little plants about 6 to 9 inches in height. This species has a reputation of not being long-lived, and is best treated as a rock garden plant.
Sources: 3,32

S. lucida — Very similar to the above in size, recommended treatment, and life span. The flowers are more lilac than blue.
Source: 57

S. graminifolia — Grassleaf Scabiosa — Silvery grass-like foliage on 10-inch plants. The flowers are pinkish and appear from June into August. Another species that is best in the rock garden.
Sources: 13,24,32; C,I

| *Sedum spectabile* | Showy Stone Crop, Live-Forever |
| | Crassula Family (Crassulaceae) |

There are many species in the genus *Sedum* for use in the rock garden, but only two are subjects for the low maintenance flower border. Of the two, the one that should have a home in every border is the nearly indestructible *S. spectabile*, the Showy Stone Crop.

This forms a neat, compact mound about 18 inches high, and produces numerous brightly colored flowers in large flat-headed clusters (cymes) 3 to 6 inches across from early August until frost. Another species quite similar in appearance and uses is *S. telephium* (called Live-Forever or Orpine).

These two require a well-drained soil in full sun. Division will not be necessary for many years, and the plants need be disturbed only when an increase is desired. They are best seen as single specimens, or in small groups of no more than three, planted about 15 inches apart at the front of the border.

S. spectabile — Showy Stone Crop — Rosy pink flowers.
Sources: 58,66,68; B

S. spectabile 'Brilliant' — Carmine flowers.
Sources: 13,20,24,37,61,66,68; C,H,I,J,K,L,M

S. spectabile 'Carmen' — Carmine-rose to red flowers.
Sources: 28,32,66,67; L

S. spectabile 'Meteor' — Very large wine-red flower clusters.
Sources: 13,32,66,67; C

S. spectabile 'Star Dust' — Ivory-white flowers. Blue-green leaves.
Sources: 13,24,32,49,69,70; C,I

S. telephium 'Indian Chief' — Copper or Indian-red flowers. Gray-green leaves.
Sources: 24,32,66,67,68; A,F,I,L

Above and below: Sedum spectabile

Above: Sidalcea 'Stark's Hybrids'

S. telephium 'Autumn Joy' — Rust-brown flowers.
Sources: 28,32,49,66,69; L

Sidalcea   **Prairie Mallow, Miniature Hollyhock**
Hibiscus Family (Malvaceae)

Here is an answer, in diminutive form, for those who wish a
Hollyhock-like plant without the biennial characteristics of the
true Hollyhock. Prairie Mallows are the products of cross breeding several western American species to obtain a group of narrow upright plants about 3 feet in height with flowers in bright
shades of rose, pink or purple. They have single flowers, and
the same vertical effect as Hollyhocks, but the leaves are deeply

lobed, quite unlike those of Hollyhocks. Another dissimilarity is the freedom from infestations of Hollyhock rust.

Sidalceas require a position in full sun and must have a good well-drained loamy soil that is moisture retentive in summer, but well drained in the winter. They are excellent subjects for the middle of the border when planted in small groups with 12 to 15-inch spacings. Division of the clumps after the fourth year is advisable. Cutting back the plants immediately after flowering in July will encourage second flowering at the end of the summer.

S. 'Elsie Heugh' — Soft pink flowers. Plants 2 to 3 feet in height.
Source: 68

S. 'Rose Queen' — Rose-pink flowers. Plants about 4 feet in height.
Source: 66

S. 'Rosy Gem' — Rose-pink flowers. Plants 1½ to 3 feet in height.
Source: 69

S. 'Stark's Hybrids' — Mixture of pink, white or purplish varieties. Plants 3 feet in height.
Sources: 13,24,68; C,I

Solidago   **Goldenrod**
                                        Daisy Family (Compositae)
Goldenrods are such conspicuous "weeds" of the wayside from midsummer to fall that their garden value is overlooked in this country. Perhaps, too, they are spurned because of their undeserved reputation as hay fever plants.

Hybridization involving several of our native species, principally in Europe, has produced cultivars with 10 to 12-inch flower heads on compact plants. They are first class perennial border subjects.

Full sun is necessary, and almost any soil type except the extremes will do. There are no significant insect or disease problems, plants are extremely hardy, and staking is not required. Division after the fourth year of flowering is frequently necessary. Plants appear best in groups of three, spaced about 12 inches apart.

S. 'Cloth of Gold' — Soft Primrose-yellow flowers in large clusters, on compact plants 18 to 20 inches in height. Mid-August and September.
Sources: 32,67

S. 'Golden Mosa' — Dark yellow flowers on plants 3 feet in height. August and September.
Sources: 13,24,67,69; C,I

S. 'Leraft' — Bright golden-yellow flowers on plants 3 feet in height. August.
Sources: 13,24,69; C,I

S. 'Peter Pan' — Canary-yellow flowers on plants 2½ feet in height. August.
Sources: 32,67

Stachys   Betony, Lamb's Ears
                                          Mint Family (Labiatae)
The two recommended species in this group differ so greatly in appearance that they are discussed separately below. They have similar cultural requirements that include a position in full sun and very well-drained soil of moderate fertility. They require no care other than occasional division sometime after the fourth year depending upon the condition of the plants.

S. macrantha — Big Betony (may sometimes be listed as *Betonica grandiflora*, but is most commonly found in catalogs as *Stachys grandiflora*) — This grows to a height of 1½ to 2 feet and produces tiered whorls of typical Mint-like, 1-inch bright purple flowers. These appear in May and June and are excellent as cut flowers. The heart-shaped leaves are wrinkled and hairy. This species will tolerate partial shade and in such a position the flowers may last longer.
Sources: 67,68

S. lanata — Woolly Betony — This is a wonderful low plant for a silvery foliage effect. Its soft, gray, densely hairy, tongue-shaped leaves are 4 to 6 inches long. The plant forms a mat of growth often 2 feet in width and a few inches in height, but may become invasive in rich soil. The flowering stalks rise to about 12 inches above the leaves and bear small pinkish purple flowers starting in June. These continue to appear until the end

of the growing season. Although the flowers really cannot be called ugly, they are not handsome either, and some gardeners may wish to cut them off. This species has great value as an accent at the front of the border when used sparingly.
Sources: 13,24,46,49,66,67,69; A,C,E,I,L

Below: Stachys lanata. *Photo: P. Bruns.*

Stokesia laevis   Stokes Aster, Cornflower Aster
                                                  Daisy Family (Compositae)

There is only one species, which is listed invariably in catalogs under the old name *S. cyanea*. The plant is of value for its blue, 3 to 4-inch, Aster-like flowers in August and September. It is of easy culture where a well-drained soil in winter can be provided. If this is not possible, it would be better not to attempt to grow this plant in our area.

In nature the flowering stems may reach 18 to 24 inches in height but cultivated selections seldom grow more than 12 inches tall. Stokesias are most effective when planted in groups of at least three, about 12 to 15 inches apart. Spring planting or dividing is recommended. After the fourth year of flowering the plants will probably become crowded and require division.
Sources: 4,14,24,49; A,I,L

S. laevis **'Blue Danube'** — Deep blue flowers in July and August Plants 12 to 15 inches in height.
Sources: 13,24,28,49,58,60; C,I,J,K

S. laevis **'Blue Moon'** — Quite large silvery blue to lilac flowers.
Sources: 13,25,37,66,68; C,H,L

S. laevis **'Blue Star'** — Light blue flowers.
Sources: 67; B

S. laevis **'Silver Moon'** — Pure white flowers.
Sources: 13,24; C,I.

Above: Stokesia laevis

Thalictrum   **Meadowrue**
Buttercup Family (Ranunculaceae)

The delicate compound foliage and lacy flowers of the Meadowrues can be used to impart a light airy feeling in the border.
The flowers, which have no true petals, are comprised of petal-
like sepals and numerous colored stamens. This somewhat unusual characteristic seldom fails to attract attention.

Most species tolerate shady conditions, but may be grown in
full sun if soil is relatively moist. The taller growing species
have sturdy stems, so staking is seldom required. Established
plants should remain in good condition for a number of years.
Flowers are excellent for cutting. To achieve maximum effect
in the garden, set the plants in groups of at least three, spaced
15 to 18 inches apart.

T. aquilegifolium — Columbine Meadowrue — The gray-green
leaves are similar in appearance to those of the Columbine. The
individual lilac-purple flowers are small but produced in great
quantity on 3-foot stems; they appear for a relatively brief period
in late May and early June.
Sources: 32,66

Left: Stokesia laevis

***T. aquilegifolium* 'Album'** — White-flowered form.
Source: 32

***T. aquilegifolium* 'Dwarf Purple'** — Purple flowers on plants 2½ feet in height.
Sources: 24; I

***T. aquilegifolium* 'Roseum'** — Pink flowers.
Source: 32

T. dipterocarpum — Yunnan Meadowrue — Has lavender or mauve flowers with contrasting yellow stamens. A valuable plant for its August flowering. Reaches a height of about 5 feet and requires a rich moist soil. This species was discovered in Western China by Ernest H. Wilson while travelling for the Veitch Nurseries before he became associated with the Arnold Arboretum.
Sources: 24,66; I

***T. dipterocarpum* 'Album'** — White-flowered form.
Source: 68

***T. dipterocarpum* 'Hewitt's Double'** — A completely double form with rich mauve flowers, it is probably the most desirable cultivar, but does not appear to be available at present from any mail-order source in the country.

T. minus (may be found in catalogs listed by its old name, *T. adiantifolium*) — Low Meadowrue — This is a handsome foliage plant for the front of the border. The much-dissected, fern-like leaves are reminiscent of the Maiden Hair Fern, and are of great value in bouquets. The flowers appearing in June and July are greenish-yellow and not at all conspicuous.
Source: 32

T. rocquebrunianum — Lavender Mist — This is one of the finest of the Meadowrues, and a plant that could well be in every garden. The lavender flowers with soft yellow stamens appear at the top of 6-foot stems from mid-July through August. Gardeners should not be discouraged with this species after the first or even the second year, especially if the plants obtained from the nursery were small; they require a few years to come into their own.
Sources: 13,32,67; C

Thalictrum rocquebrunianum

T. speciosissimum — Dusty Meadowrue — This yellow-flowered species may be found listed in catalogs as *T. glaucum* or *T. rugosum*. The dense clusters of slightly fragrant flowers appear in August on stems 4 to 6 feet in height. The blue-gray leaves are effective in flower arrangements.
Sources: 32,66,67

Thermopsis   **False Lupine**
Pea Family (Leguminosae)
This is another in the relatively small group of perennials that have the ability to endure considerable neglect for many years. Although native in the Southeast, it will survive New England winters, has no insect or disease problems, and the compound leaves remain in excellent condition throughout the growing season. The 12-inch spikes of bright yellow, pealike flowers appearing in June and early July resemble a yellow Lupine, hence the common name.

Old plants may reach a height of 4 feet and form clumps up to a yard wide. Under such conditions they may require staking. False Lupines should be grown in full sun in soil that is well drained; only moderate fertility is necessary.
Sources: 3,4,13,14,25,29,66,68,69; B,C,E,K

Tradescantia virginiana   **Spiderwort**
Spiderwort Family (Commelinaceae)
Our native spiderwort, *Tradescantia virginiana*, is a plant that will tolerate poor soil, poor drainage and poor light, but may become a serious pest under favorable conditions. Plants reach a height of 18 to 24 inches and have fleshy, somewhat grass-like leaves and stems. The three-petaled flowers appear in small clusters during the summer.

***T. virginiana* 'Blue Stone'** — Clear deep blue flowers.
Sources: 24,69; I

***T. virginiana* 'Innocence'** — Pure white flowers.
Source: 66

***T. virginiana* 'Iris Prichard'** — White flowers with a violet flush.
Sources: 13,32,66,67,69; C

T. virginiana 'T. C. Weguelin' — Porcelain-blue flowers.
Sources: 13,24,32,66,69; C,I

T. virginiana 'Kreisler' — Deep blue flowers.
Source: 66

T. virginiana 'Orchid Lady' — Orchid-pink flowers.
Source: 1

T. virginiana 'Pauline' — Rose-mauve flowers.
Sources: 13,24,32,69; C,I,K

T. virginiana 'Pink Delight' — Rich orchid-pink flowers.
Source: 1

T. virginiana 'Purple Dome' — Rosy-purple flowers.
Sources: 13,24,32,67,68,69; C,I

T. virginiana 'Purple Perfection' — Rich purple flowers.
Source: 1

T. virginiana 'Red Cloud' — Rosy-red flowers.
Sources: 13,24,32,69; C,I,K

T. virginiana 'Royal Purple' — Deep purple flowers.
Source: 1

T. virginiana 'Snowcap' — Pure white flowers.
Sources: 13,24,32,69; C,I

T. virginiana 'Valour' — Deep red-violet flowers.
Source: 66

T. virginiana 'Zwanenburg Blue' — Medium blue flowers.
Source: 66

Trollius   **Globe Flower**
                          Buttercup Family (Ranunculaceae)
   Globe Flowers are found in nature growing in sunny, moist
or marshy situations. In the garden they must have a position
where they will remain moist throughout the summer. Under
such conditions they will require little attention for many years.
Despite catalog claims to the contrary, they bloom only in spring
and early summer.
   The flowers range in size from 2 to 3 inches and may be single
or double in shades ranging from pale yellow to orange. They
make excellent, long-lasting subjects for flower arrangements.

The deeply-lobed leaves resemble those of Buttercups. According to species or cultivar they range in height from 1 to 3 feet and are most effective in groups of at least three spaced 10 to 12 inches apart near the front or middle of the flower border. Division may be accomplished either in spring or fall, but in most situations it will not be necessary for five years or more.

Although a number of fine selections are available in this country, it is unfortunate that more nurseries do not stock them.

T. asiaticus 'Byrne's Giant' — Orange-yellow, semidouble flowers with bright orange-red anthers. Plants 2½ feet in height. Flowers a little later than the *T. europaeus* hybrids.
Source: 69

T. europaeus — Common Globe Flower — The true species probably is not offered by nurseries; but a number of cultivars attributed to this species are available. Many are undoubtedly hybrids between *T. europaeus* and other species.

T. europaeus 'Commander-in-Chief' — Large deep orange flowers. Plants about 2 feet in height. Less vigorous than most other varieties and prefers a deep, rich soil.
Source: 66

T. europaeus 'Earliest of All' — Small clear yellow flowers. Plants about 2 feet in height, true to name.
Source: 66

T. europaeus 'Excelsior' — Bright yellow flowers.
Source: 32

T. europaeus 'Fire Globe' — Deep burnished orange flowers. 2 feet.
Source: 32

T. europaeus 'First Lancers' — Fiery orange flowers. 2½ feet.
Source: 66

T. europaeus 'Golden Monarch' — Large golden-yellow flowers.
Source: 66

T. europaeus 'Lemon Queen' — Very pale lemon-yellow flowers. 2 feet.
Sources: 32,66,68; C

T. europaeus 'Mrs. Mary Russell' — Pale yellow flowers.
Sources: 66,68

T. europaeus '**Orange Glow**' — Large deep orange-yellow flowers. Sources: 32,66

T. europaeus '**Orange Princess**' — Orange-gold flowers. 2½ feet. Source: 68

T. europaeus '**Prichard's Giant**' — Large golden-yellow flowers. Plants about 2½ feet in height. Sources: 66,69; C

T. europaeus '**Superbus**' — Bright lemon-yellow flowers. Source: 68

T. ledebouri — Ledebour Globe Flower — Similar in general appearance to the preceding species, but flowering starts in June. The flowers are orange-gold with erect bright orange stamens. Plants attain a height of about 2 to 2½ feet. Sources: 14,32,37,67,68,69

T. ledebouri '**Golden Queen**' — This is the tallest of all the *Trollius* cultivars, reaching a height of nearly 4 feet under the most favorable circumstances. The very large flowers, often 4 inches across, are orange-yellow. Sources: C,I

T. pumilus — Dwarf Globe Flower — This is a treasure for a moist spot on the rock garden or similar situation at the very front of the flower border. The 1-inch, clear yellow flowers are produced in May and June on plants 6 to 8 inches in height. Source: 29

Verbascum   Mullein
Figwort Family (Scrophulariaceae)
Although they are close relatives of the common Mullein, V. *thapsus*, which is frequently seen along roadsides and in waste places in our area, the species and cultivars for garden use **far** outshine the wild plant. Unfortunately the types most frequently available to the gardening public exhibit biennial tendencies, and new batches of seedlings must be raised every year to insure against losses. Many of the species and cultivars will self-sow and perpetuate themselves in a low maintenance situation, but this cannot always be guaranteed.

The key to success with *Verbascum* is a location where the soil is very well drained especially during the winter months. Sandy loam that has moderate fertility will suffice, but the planting site must be in full sun. Although plants will withstand surprising amounts of drought, periodic watering during long dry spells will be beneficial.

The types discussed here vary in height from 2 to 4 feet. The five-petaled saucer-shaped flowers are about an inch in width and densely borne on spikes above basal rosettes of green to silvery-gray leaves. Depending upon variety, the spikes may be solitary or branched; some types produce numerous secondary spikes. The taller varieties invariably need staking to prevent the flower spikes from bending or flopping over after heavy rain. Removal of the flowering stalks immediately after flowering may encourage the production of new basal rosettes of foliage, thus discouraging the biennial tendencies of some of the forms. This will not always work, however.

V. nigrum — Dark Mullein — This European native bears bold 2 to 3-foot spikes of small yellow flowers that are purplish at the center. The basal leaves may be oblong or heart-shaped. This species will often be much longer lived than the others discussed here.
Source: 69

V. nigrum var. *album* — White-flowered form of the above species.
Sources: 24; I

V. phoeniceum — Purple Mullein — This species exhibits a strong biennial tendency. It is one of the principal parents of the garden hybrids, and unfortunately that tendency has been passed along to them. In a sunny dry location, the plant self-sows with little difficulty in the Boston area, but not prolifically. Plants reach a height of 2½ to 3 feet and bear loosely branched spikes of ¾-inch white to violet or purple flowers.
Sources: 66,69; L

V. × *hybridum* 'Bridal Bouquet' — Pure white flowers on plants 2½ to 3 feet in height.
Source: 66

V. × *hybridum* 'Cotswold Gem' — Soft amber-colored flowers with purple centers. Plants 3 to 4 feet in height.
Sources: 24,67,69; I

V. × *hybridum* 'Pink Domino' — Rose-pink flowers with maroon centers. Plants 4 feet in height.
Sources: 13,24,66,69; C,I

V. × *hybridum* 'Yellow Queen' — Bright yellow flowers on plants 3 feet in height.
Source: 68

Veronica   Speedwell
Figwort Family (Scrophulariaceae)
This is a very large group of garden plants. Many are best

suited to the rock garden or naturalized areas, but a surprisingly large number of forms of great value in the perennial garden are presently offered by American nurseries. Of these selections, most are suitable for a low maintenance situation and are highly prized for their flowers which are excellent for cutting. Blue predominates, but purple, white and pink shades are obtainable as well. With proper selection of varieties, a succession of bloom throughout most of the growing season is possible.

The flowers are small, but are borne densely on numerous erect spikes. Plants vary in height, according to variety, from 12 to 18 inches. They do best in an open, airy, sunny location where the soil is of moderate fertility and well drained, especially during the winter. For tidy growth, clumps probably will require division after the fourth year, either in the spring or fall. Single specimens, or small groups of three plants spaced 12 to 18 inches apart at the front or towards the middle of the border are equally satisfactory.

V. holophylla — Japanese Speedwell — Broad spikes about 12 to 15 inches high with vivid blue flowers. Starts to bloom in August and continues almost to the end of the growing season. Deep green glossy foliage. Very hardy.
Sources: 13,24,29,32; C,I

V. incana — Woolly Speedwell — The woolly white leaves and lilac-blue flowers form a handsome contrast. The flowers appear on 12 to 18-inch stems in June and July. When not in flower the plants seldom exceed 6 inches in height, so may be used at the front of the border or in the rock garden as well. Good drainage is a necessity.
Sources: 14,24,39,46,49,66,68,69; A,I,J,K,L

V. latifolia — Hungarian Speedwell — This species forms a tangled mound of foliage. The deep blue flowers are produced with surprising freedom throughout most of the summer.
Source: 66

V. latifolia 'Crater Lake Blue' — A most desirable cultivar of the above species. It has vivid gentian-blue flowers and the same long blooming season.
Sources: 24,32,59,66,67,69; I,K

V. longifolia — Beach Speedwell, Clump Speedwell — Densely borne, lilac-blue flowers on long spikes that average 2 feet in height. Flowers from midsummer to fall.
Sources: 66; L

V. longifolia* var. *subsessilis — Rich royal blue flowers, quite striking in their effect. Much superior to the species form, and with the same long blooming period.
Sources: 24,46,66,67; B,I

V. spicata — Spike Speedwell — Numerous 14 to 18-inch dense spikes of bright blue flowers from June to early August.
Sources: 30; K,L

V. spicata* var. *alba — Pure white-flowered form of the preceding species.
Source: 66

***V. spicata* 'Nana'** — A very low compact form not over 6 inches in height. Probably of more value in the rock garden, but of some interest for the very front of the flower border. Blue flowers at the same time as the species.
Source: 66

***V. spicata* 'Nana Alba'** — White-flowered form of the above cultivar.
Source: 66

Of the following list of cultivars, some may properly belong under *V. spicata* and others under *V. longifolia*. The two species have been crossed extensively and some cultivars are obviously hybrids between the two. For convenience they are lumped together here as *Veronica* hybrids.

V. 'Barcarolle' — 1-foot spikes of striking deep rose-pink flowers from June to August.
Sources: 24,49,59,69; I,K

V. 'Blue Champion' — Medium blue flowers from July to late summer on bushy, 2½-foot plants.
Source: 67

V. 'Blue Peter' — Deep blue flowers on compact spikes. Much branched 1½-foot plants with fairly long serrated leaves. Blooms from July to August.
Sources: 68,69; B,I

V. 'Blue Spire' — Very erect 1½-foot plants with deep violet-blue flowers from June to August.
Sources: 13,66; C

V. 'Icicle' — Pure white flowers from June to September on 2-

foot spikes. Gray-green leaves.
Sources: 13,14,24,32,39,46,58,66,67,68,69; C,I,J,K,L

V. **'Lavender Charm'** — Lavender-blue flowers on 18 to 24-inch spikes from June to September. Dark glossy green leaves.
Sources: 13,24; C,I,J

V. **'Minuet'** — Soft pink flowers from June to August on plants about 1 foot in height. Handsome gray-green foliage.
Sources: 13,14,24,32,39,46,49,66,67; C,I,J,K,L

V. **'Pavane'** — Bright pink or rose flowers from June to August on 18-inch spikes.
Sources: 32,58,66; K

V. **'Pink Spire'** — 18 to 24-inch spikes of soft pink flowers with red anthers. Gray-green foliage.
Sources: 13,66; C

V. **'Romily Purple'** — Dark blue-violet flowers from June to August on rigid spikes 1½ to 2 feet in height.
Source: 68

V. **'Saraband'** — Violet-blue flowers from June through August on 20-inch spikes.
Sources: 66,67

V. **'Sunny Border Blue'** — Navy-blue flowers from June to September on 18 to 24-inch spikes.
Sources: 13; C,J,L

Although all of the following are excellent in their own way, they are quite low growing and not superior to the few low types already mentioned. For this reason it is suggested that they are better suited to the rock garden than to the front of the flower border.

V. alpina 'Alba' — White flowers on stalks seldom exceeding 6 to 8 inches in height.
Sources: 24,67,69; I

V. pectinata 'Rosea' — A mat-forming plant with pink flowers with white centers. Hardiness a bit doubtful in the Boston area.
Source: 66

V. prostrata (sometimes listed in catalogs as *V. rupestris*) — Harebell Speedwell — Forms tufted mats of foliage. Flower spikes 2 to 8 inches in height. Flowers deep blue in May and June.
Sources: 68; B

***V. prostrata* 'Heavenly Blue'** — Sapphire-blue flowers, otherwise the same as the above.
Sources: 24; I,K

V. repens — Creeping Speedwell — Plants 2 inches in height produce slender spikes of pale or lavender blue flowers in June.
Sources: 32,66; A

HARDY ORNAMENTAL GRASSES

Some of the easiest perennials to grow are members of the Grass family (*Gramineae*). They are not seen frequently enough in perennial gardens, and some have a special importance in a low maintenance situation. Ornamental grasses may be of value for their habit of growth, variegated leaves, or decorative inflorescences (flowers). Most possess combinations of these; with some, winter interest is an added asset. The dried flowers or fruiting stalks of many are useful in flower arrangements as well.

All the grasses recommended here are fully hardy in our area and should grow for many years before division for rejuvenation will be necessary. This is best done in early spring, just before new growth commences, and only when clumps start to die out in the center. Those noted for their winter interest should be allowed to retain their dead leaves until early spring, at which time plants should be cut back to an inch or so above ground level.

An excellent, fully illustrated publication *Ornamental Grasses for the Home and Garden*, Information Bulletin 64, is available at a price of $.30 from the Extension Service, New York State College of Agriculture and Life Sciences, Cornell University, Ithaca, New York, 14850.

***Carex morrowi* 'Variegata'** — Japanese Sedge Grass — A low, clump forming plant (actually a sedge, Cyperaceae, not a true grass) that grows from 6 to 12 inches in height. The evergreen leaves have narrow white margins. The flowers are insignificant. It will not spread rapidly under normal conditions and is handsome in both winter and summer. Full sun or partial shade is satisfactory, but a soil that does not dry out for long periods is necessary. Excellent for growing in pots or other containers, both indoors and out.
Sources: 66,67; C

Elymus glaucus — Blue Lime Grass — A very densely-tufted grass with short blue-green leaves. It grows to a height of about 2 feet and is quite effective in small groupings at the front of the border. Unlike *E. arenarius* which is sometimes used in gardens, this species does not spread rapidly. Full sun is necessary, but the soil may be either moist or sandy and fairly dry. Useful in gardens near the sea. The leaves lose their coloration with the first frost.
Sources: 66; L

Erianthus ravennae — Plume Grass, Ravenna Grass, Hardy Pampas Grass — This is a very stately, tall grass that forms imposing 5-foot clumps, and flowering stalks rising 7 to 10 feet in height. It gives the closest effect to Pampas Grass of any plant that can be easily grown in New England. The green leaves present a somewhat coarse effect. The silvery plumes of white or beige flowers are 1 to 2 feet long and appear in September and early October. These are occasionally destroyed by early frosts. Well-established clumps may produce upwards of 40 to 50 flower heads and these are excellent for use in dried arrangements.

Plume Grass is not invasive, but clumps do eventually become several feet in width. A single specimen will be sufficient in most gardens, where the effect will be dramatic to say the least. Where massed, it can be effective as screening for those who may wish something a bit out of the ordinary. Foliage should not be cut down until early spring as the plants have a rather handsome effect in winter. A fairly moist but well-drained and fertile soil should be provided along with full sun.
Sources: 67; B

Miscanthus sinensis (syn. *Eulalia japonica*) — Eulalia Grass, Chinese Silver Grass — This is another very tall grass, usually attaining heights of 5 to 10 feet, and has many of the same uses as *Erianthus ravennae* due to its large size. The flowers are pale pink or red and appear in large, feathery fan-shaped panicles in September. These can be very effective when dried for arrangements. As with *Erianthus* the foliage should be left over winter and not cut until early spring. In a low maintenance situation, a site in full sun with somewhat poor but moist soil conditions should be chosen. In shady locations, or if encouraged by excessive fertility, clumps may require tying to prevent toppling.
Sources: 66; B. (The same sources list a form that they call Gigantea; this grows a foot or so taller than the species.)

Above: Clump of Miscanthus sinensis *provides a contrast to shapes and textures of shrubs and perennials in the Low Maintenance Garden at the Case Estates, Weston. Photo: P. Bruns.*

Above: Erianthus ravenne. *From Dictionnaire Practique D'Horticulture et du Jardinage. Paris, 1892–93.*

Left: Miscanthus sinensis. *From Manual of the Grasses of the U.S. (ed. 2) by A. S. Hitchcock and A. Chase. USDA Misc. Publ. 200, 1950.*

Miscanthus sinensis 'Gracillimus' — Maiden Grass — This form differs from the above in that the leaves are finer in texture, have a conspicuous white midvein and a more arching habit of growth. It is shorter by about 2 feet.
Sources: 13,24,28,67,68; B,I,L

Miscanthus sinensis 'Variegatus' — Striped Eulalia Grass — Grows to a height of 3 to 6 feet. The leaves are striped yellow, white, and green. Although hardy in the Boston area, it seldom flowers here.
Sources: 66,67; B

Miscanthus sinensis 'Zebrinus' — Zebra Grass — A very striking grass with basically green leaves that have prominent yellow bands. It has an upright habit, and the unique foliage makes it an interesting and unusual specimen plant. It is frequently used near water. Does not form as vigorous clumps as the species, and will require staking if grown in the shade.
Sources: 66,67; B

Molinea caerulea 'Variegata' — Variegated Moor Grass — This forms small dense, upright to arching tufts 1 to 2 feet in height. The leaves have cream-colored margins. The green to purplish flowers are produced over most of the summer and are effective when dried. The plant dies to the ground in winter, so has no value at that time of year. It is effective as a low specimen plant or in small groupings at the front of the border. Adapts well either to full sun or partial shade.
Sources: 24,66,69; I

Panicum virgatum — Switch Grass — Densely upright clumps 3 to 6 feet in height that produce light, airy panicles of dark reddish-purple flowers from July to September. Because of the habit of growth, Switch Grass has distinct ornamental winter value and also has been suggested for use as a wildlife cover at that time of the year. It is suitable as a specimen plant at the middle of the border, and can be used in naturalizing schemes, in waterside plantings, or as a screen when massed.

Prefers a site in full sun and is impartial to soil type. In a shady location plants may require staking. Light sandy soils may encourage spreading, but this happens slowly.
Sources: 66; B

Uniola latifolia — Northern Sea Oats, Spangle Grass — This is one of the best hardy native grasses, and probably the most appropriate for a partially shaded location. It has a narrow, upright to arching habit of growth. Clumps reach 3 to 5 feet in

Above: Panicum virgatum. *From* Yearbook of Agriculture, 1948. *U.S. Govt. Printing Office.*

Above: Uniola latifolia. *From* Manual of the Grasses of the U.S. (*ed. 2*) *by A. S. Hitchcock and A. Chase. USDA. Misc. Publ. 200, 1950.*

height. The handsome 10 to 12-inch spikes of reddish-brown flowers (which turn to bronze) appear in late July and persist into the winter when they retain their pleasing appearance. The best planting site is where soil is fertile and well drained. A position in full sun will cause the plants to grow shorter and be less effective.

Source: B

The following grasses may be used in a low maintenance situation, but they must be placed second in value to those discussed above:

Arrhenatherum elatius var. *bulbosum* 'Variegatum' — Variegated Bulbous Oat Grass, Variegated Tuber Oat Grass — This grows to a height of 18 to 25 inches and has wide green leaf blades with contrasting white stripes. The foliage is most effective in spring and autumn. Because the clumps become untidy looking during hot weather, they should be cut back to the base in midsummer. Plants have a definite tendency to spread, and possess an open, upright habit of growth. Will grow well either in full sun or partial shade, and tolerate dry soil conditions.
Sources: 24,66; I

Phalaris arundinacea 'Picta' — Ribbon Grass, Gardener's Garters — Although this is a very attractive low grass, it has a decided tendency to become rampant in light soils. Also, the foliage becomes less decorative toward the end of the summer. It grows about 2 or sometimes 3 feet in height and has an open, upright habit, not forming tight clumps or mounds. The leaves are green, striped with white, and occasionally pink. This grass was very popular in the past, and still frequently marks the site of old gardens.

Spartina pectinata 'Aureo-marginata' (syn. *S. michauxiana* 'Aureo-marginata') — Cord Grass — An excellent plant for either sandy or wet soils, but may become invasive in the former situation. It grows to a height of 4 to 8 feet (tallest in moist locations) and should have a site in full sun. The 2 to 4-foot leaves are shiny green with yellow stripes along the margins. Yellow flowers on 6 to 15-inch stalks appear from late August through September. This is a very good plant for use along streams and ponds or near the sea; it is of less value in the perennial garden.
Sources: 66; B

The following grasses are not recommended, especially in a low maintenance situation:

Arundo donax — Giant Reed — A very coarse, but striking plant. It may vary in height from 7 to 20 feet, but is seldom over 8 to 12 feet in our area. Although it can be used locally, it is at the margin of its hardiness, and must be heavily mulched in winter.
Sources: 67; B

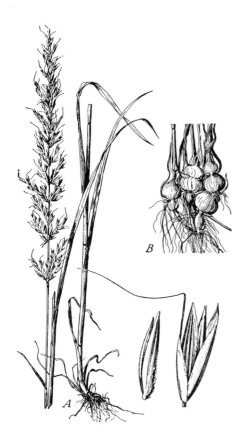

Above: Arrhenatherum elatius. *From Manual of the Grasses of the U.S. (ed. 2) by A. S. Hitchcock and A. Chase. USDA. Misc. Publ. 200, 1950.*

Reed canarygrass

Above: Phalaris arundinacea. *From Yearbook of Agriculture, 1948. U.S. Govt. Printing Office.*

Arundo donax 'Variegata' — Leaves with broad white stripes at the margins, and a narrower white stripe down the midrib. Less hardy than the species and not for outdoor culture around Boston.
Sources: 13,66,67; C

Cortaderia argentea (syn. *C. selloana*) — Pampas Grass — A densely tufted perennial grass that grows up to 9 feet and more in height and produces conspicuous silvery-white panicles of flowers in late summer. In the Boston area it can only be grown with considerable protection, and this is hardly worthwhile, as *Erianthus ravennae* makes such a good substitute.
Sources: 25,44,59; A

[194]

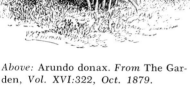

Above: Arundo donax. *From* The Garden, *Vol. XVI:322, Oct. 1879.*

Above: Festuca ovina. *From* Yearbook of Agriculture, 1948. *U.S. Govt. Printing Office.*

Festuca ovina* var. *glauca — Blue Fescue — Although this is the ornamental grass most frequently offered by nurseries, it is one of the least satisfactory for the true low maintenance situation because of its need for division every second or third year to maintain the vigor of the clumps. It is frequently suggested for use as a ground cover, a purpose to which it is unsuited. Growing in neat clumps about 6 to 12 inches in height, with silvery blue, finely textured leaves, Blue Fescue remains completely evergreen in New England winters. It must have a well-drained soil, but will tolerate either full sun or partial shade. It is a beautiful little plant, well loved by some landscape architects, but not worthwhile for easy maintenance.
Sources: 24,32,44,49,58,59,66,67; A,B,C,I,K,L

Planning and Preparing the Garden

Site Considerations

The ideal site for a perennial garden is one exposed to full sun for the entire day, out of the wind, with a well-drained, fertile, loamy soil abundantly supplied with organic matter, on flat, not sloping land, and occupying a conspicuous location on the property. Few people are blessed with such a site! Fortunately, many perennials adapt to a fairly wide range of conditions, and there are numerous species for special situations.

A thorough survey of one's property should be taken before any decision is made on location. If at all possible, the garden should be sited so that it is visible either from the house or patio, or from the street as an embellishment to the dwelling itself.

Traditionally the perennial garden has been provided with a backdrop, usually a hedge or wall of some sort. Wooden and metal fences of many styles are used for this purpose; in fact, a well-planned perennial border can mask a chain link fence as effectively as it complements the beauty of a wooden fence or screen. Other backdrops may include the shrubbery in the foundation planting of a house, a wall of the house itself, or the boundary of a woodland using the distant scene as a backdrop.

Today landscape thinking and practice have set the perennial border free of the prescribed, often stereotyped, backdrop, making it optional according to the situation. The garden now may be brought out into the middle of the lawn, independent of any single feature, yet integrated into the total scene. In such a position it can take on the various shapes of free-form beds often raised or contoured, and gently defined by curving lines. Shrubs having contrasting shapes, textures, or color can be used as complementary plantings; even interesting large stones or boulders may be sparingly incorporated. The use of these elements adds extra interest during both the growing season and the bleak winter months when most gardens are least attractive.

Liberation from the necessity of providing a riot of color at all times enables the gardener to give consideration to the subtleties of texture and leaf form, to the dramatic effects of bold masses, or interesting small nooks set against the lines or shape of the garden itself. Freed from the rectangular or circular designs that any child could produce, the art rather than the trade of horticulture can come into full play, and almost endless possibilities for the design or location of beds and borders can arise: beside walks, along driveways, in or next to terraces or patios, around existing specimen shrubs or small trees, at the base of a rock outcropping, with or partially surrounding the vegetable garden, by a fence or hedge, or amongst the shrubs of the foundation planting. The number of acceptable sites for perennials, and for low maintenance perennials in particular, is almost equal to the diverse sites to be found on any property.

Sun vs. Shade

Once a visually satisfying location for the perennial garden is selected, attention must be given to the interrelated factors of soil and sun and shade. A relatively large number of plants will survive a poor dry soil in full sun; but relatively few will do well in deep shade even with soil of optimum quality.

Shade conditions may be divided into three categories: 1) partial shade, 2) light shade, and 3) deep shade. Partial shade exists when a location is in direct sun for only a portion of each day. Many sun-loving perennials will adapt to such conditions, but the fewer the hours of direct sun, the greater will be the need for staking, the greater the danger from fungus diseases, and the likelihood that some plants will produce rampant growth. Full sun during the early or later hours of the day is sometimes considered to be preferable to full sun during the middle of the day. Early afternoon sun is the hottest, and is apt to dry the soil and cause flowers to fade rapidly.

Light shade exists when plants receive no direct sunlight, but the light intensity is nonetheless high. This occurs when widely spaced buildings or trees cut off the direct rays of the sun, and is the ideal condition for nearly all shade-loving plants. The extreme condition, deep shade, results when plants receive no direct sunlight, and the light intensity is quite low, similar to indoor room conditions. In such a situation, root competition from trees is often a serious problem. As a practical rule of thumb, the roots of a tree extend from the trunk at least as far as the tips of the branches. A garden that is situated beneath the branches of a tree has to contend with not only the lack of light produced by the branches, but also the competition of the tree roots for water and nutrients. If at all possible a perennial garden should not be sited adjacent to trees.

Soil and Its Modifications

Existing soil conditions may limit choice of perennials just as exposure to varying degrees of light can affect success. Though it frequently is not possible to alter exposure to sun or shade, soils can be modified; perennials that are not to be divided frequently and will stay in place for several years or longer require thorough attention to their needs *before* they are planted.

The first order of business is to determine what is under the surface of the soil. One or more holes should be dug to a depth of 18 to 24 inches in the area of the prospective site. This will determine the depth of the topsoil, the character of the subsoil, and the conditions of drainage. Many housing developments provide only an inch or two of top soil over a gravel or clay subsoil. This is not adequate to support a garden. Furthermore, the subsoil may be contaminated with mortar, old boards, tin cans, broken bottles, and similar debris that will interfere with drainage and nutrient availability.

The soil for the perennial garden should be 6 to 8 inches deep; the subsoil should be freely drained, and drainage should not be impeded by a layer of clay (hardpan). If the conditions are not ideal, they can be easily remedied. The amount and depth of the soil can be increased by incorporating some sort of organic material into the top 6 to 8 inches. This may be compost, stable or cow manure, sawdust, leaves, chopped hay; in short, any sort of decomposable organic matter that can be obtained cheaply. It can be incorporated into the soil with a rototiller, or it can be dug in with a fork or shovel. Preferably, it should be dug in several months before planting is contemplated to allow time for decomposition. Organic matter also will help moisture retention in a droughty, sandy or gravelly soil, and will tend to lighten a clay soil. However, if drainage is poor, it will pay to add sufficient bulk to the soil to raise the surface several inches above the surroundings. Always the watchword is organic matter and more organic matter.

It is impossible to state how much fertilizer or lime should be added to the soil before planting. That depends entirely upon the existing state of fertility, and it is necessary to have a soil test made to obtain the true picture. Most State Experiment Stations or County Extension Services will make such tests and distribute information on how to collect a proper sample for analysis. The report they issue on the analysis will state how much of a particular fertilizer will be needed for so many square feet, how much lime will be required to compensate for over-acidity (most perennials prefer soil conditions ranging from slightly on the acid side to near neutral), and how much organic matter will be needed. Fertilizer and lime are easily purchased in any garden store. If the garden is being prepared in the autumn, to be planted the following spring, it is best to with-hold fertilizer until spring and rototill again.

Initial preparation of a new site is usually best in the autumn. The soil is easier to work then; grass can be rototilled in to decompose over the winter, and the soil has a chance to settle. If the initial preparation is in the spring, the grass should be removed, including all roots, and placed on the compost pile. After rototilling the soil will be too loose for immediate plant-ing. It should be tamped down by slightly treading with the feet, up and down in rows until the entire area is covered. A distinction should be made here between "treading" and "stomp-ing" as it is easy to compact the soil too much, especially if it is wet. After the treading process is completed, and a firm planting bed has been established, the soil should be raked level, and the planting process may begin.

After the garden has been planted it should be mulched to a depth of 2 to 4 inches with the same material that was dug in to provide organic matter. This mulch should be renewed an-nually. In the long run a mulch should break down and add organic matter and nutrients to the soil; in the short run, it re-duces the temperature of the soil in the summer, delays freezing in the fall and warming in the spring (thus helping to avoid frost damage), and acts as a reservoir for soil moisture. It also slows evaporation of water from the soil surface, and inhibits the germination of weed seeds in the soil. Proprietary mulching materials such as ground bark may be used, but they have little to commend them over less expensive materials. Peatmoss has disadvantages since it dries to form a surface that is difficult to wet; on the other hand, once thoroughly wet it may cause soggy soil conditions.

Some Suggested Staking Methods

The tendency to flop, or the inability of a plant to bear the heavy weight of its own flowers has been listed throughout this handbook as a "fault" possessed by a number of perennials. Some that have this unfortunate tendency possess too many other good characteristics to be excluded from the low maintenance garden.

All methods illustrated here are simple, effective, and require very little time of the hurried gardener. It should be emphasized, however, that all staking should be done as early in the growing season as possible, or as soon as the taller growing plants have attained half their height.

Staking a full grown plant requires much more time, and results frequently are unattractive. If it is allowed to flop, or to be toppled by wind and rain, stems often can become twisted or sometimes broken. After a few days the twists tend to become permanent, and staking at such a late date is of very little benefit.

Below: A clump of Thermopsis *has collapsed at the end of the summer. Proper staking earlier in the growing season would have prevented this problem.*

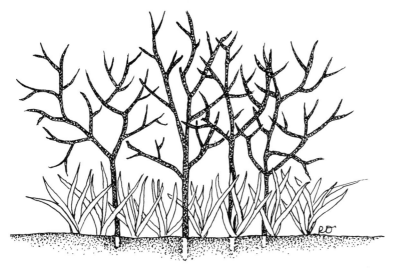

Many plants that produce multiple stems may be staked with small twiggy branches set in the ground just as, or even before, plants commence growth in the spring. This is an old European method, particularly favored with Asters. Seldom used in this country, it is most effective.

As the plant grows, it is completely supported by the twigs, but the twigs are entirely hidden.

The stems of some taller perennials with large, heavy flowers must be staked individually. Green bamboo canes are best with such plants as *Delphinium* and the larger flowered Chrysanthemums; Raffia, cloth or plastic ties are preferred to metal or wire ties which may constrict or damage stems. A twist in the tie should be made between the stem of the plant and the stake to further avoid damage to the stem.

Shorter plants such as Peonies with large, heavy flowers can be supported with a round hoop attached to three or four legs. Such hoops are easily constructed from heavy gauge wire or even old coat hangers. The legs may be either of wire or bamboo cane.

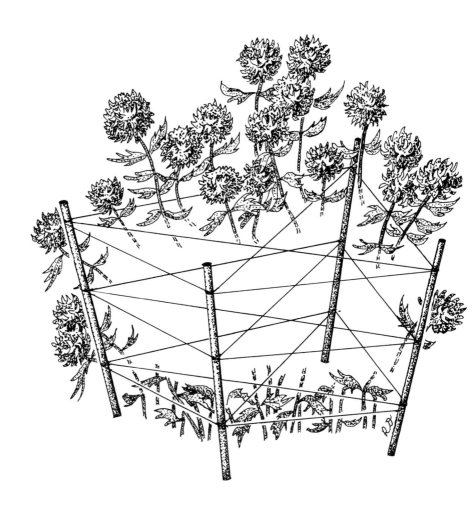

Many taller perennials form dense clumps with many stems. With such plants the most satisfactory method of support is often to construct a "cage" with bamboo canes and string as shown in the diagram. If this is done relatively early in the growing season, the structure will be almost completely hidden by the subsequent growth of the plant.

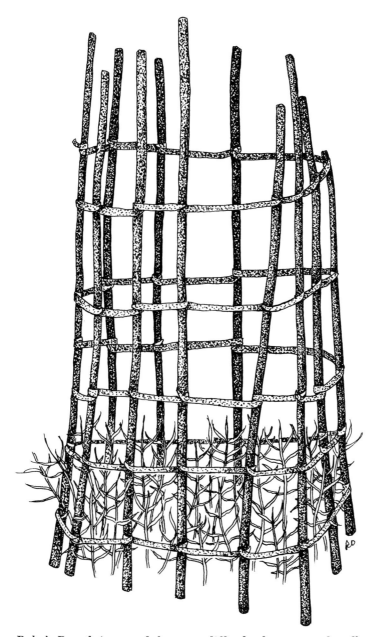

Baby's Breath is one of the most difficult plants to stake effectively. The method we offer is pictured in the White Flower Farm catalog and adapted here.

Just as growth starts, 10 to 12 bamboo canes about 2 feet high are placed all around the clump. Twist-Ems are then used to make rings around the canes.

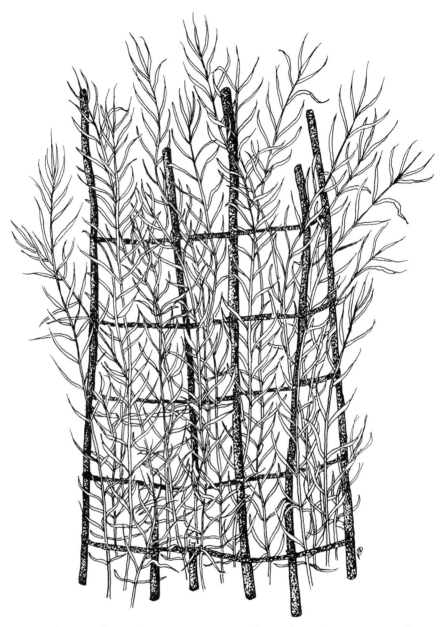

As growth progresses, stems grow through, and are supported
by the structure.

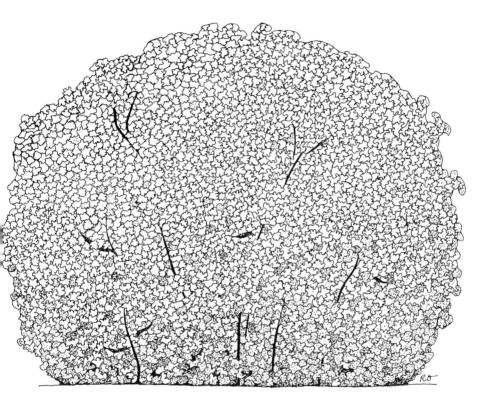

By the time the plant flowers, the supporting structure is
completely hidden and the plant will withstand high winds or
rain without injury.

Division

Sooner or later most perennials will need to be divided — either to prevent excessive spreading, or to reinvigorate the plant (or both). Division is also one of the simplest means of propagating many perennials on a modest scale.

Spring or fall division is satisfactory with most types. However, plants divided in the early spring just as new growth is about to start have the advantage of an entire season for new roots to grow and plants to become established before winter.

The best indications that a plant should be divided include: 1) vigor shows a general decline; 2) clumps become very tangled in growth — or become invaded by other plants and weeds; 3) clumps open up and form a dead space in the center.

The best divisions are usually obtained from the outermost portions of old clumps — i.e. growth furthest away from the center. This is the most active growing and vigorous part of the plant.

Small plants may be lifted with a fork or small spade; they also may be pulled apart by hand or cut with a knife. Three to five "eyes" constitute the best sized division. Anything smaller may not flower during the current season.

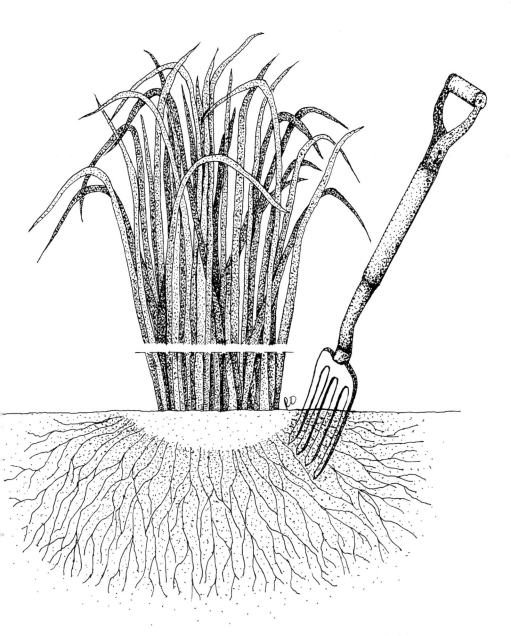

Large vigorous clumps are best lifted with a spading fork. First the top growth is cut down to about 3 inches. The fork is then inserted at several points around the outside of the clump, and gentle upward pressure exerted at each point. If this is done gradually and gently, the clump can be lifted with a minimum of root breakage.

Left: A clump of Anthemis *has died at the center and should be divided.*

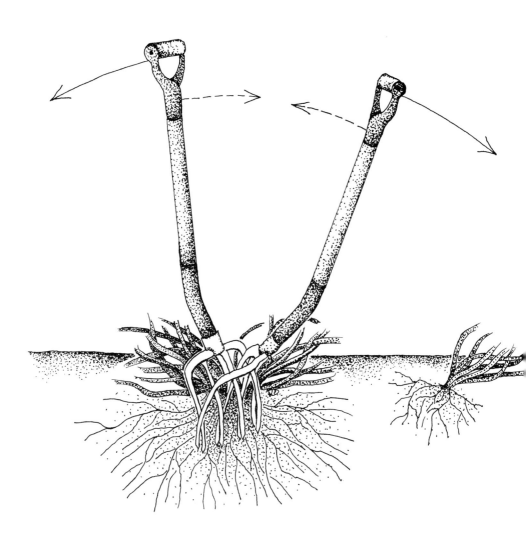

To divide large tightly growing clumps after they have been lifted, plunge one fork down through the center of the clump. Then insert a second fork parallel to the first. As indicated, pull the two forks first inward, then outward, and the clump will break in two with minimal crown and root damage. It is important that the initial placement of the forks be as shown.

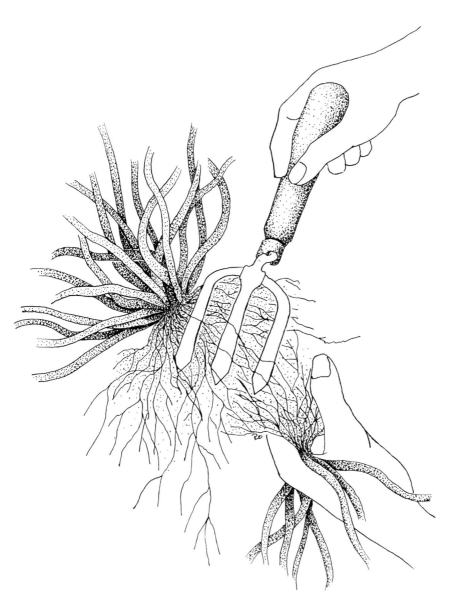

Once a large clump has been broken up by the spading forks, smaller divisions may be obtained using a hand fork or a knife.

Tabular List of Plants Mentioned

[(x) indicates the characteristic may be highly variable]

	Dry Soil Conditions	Moist Soil Conditions	Intolerant of Wet Soil in Winter	Short-lived	Invasive	Hardiness Problems (Summer Heat)	Hardiness Problems (Winter Cold)	Serious Insect or Disease Problems	For Full Sun	Partial Shade	Require Frequent Division
Achillea	x		x		(x)				x		(Every year)
Aconitum		x							x	x	
Adenophora	x	x	x				(x)		x		
Alchemilla	x	x							x	x	
Althaea		x		x	(x)			x	x		
Alyssum	x		x	(x)					x	x	
Amsonia	x	x							x		
Anaphalis	x		x						x		
Anchusa		x		x	x				x		Every other year
Anemone × hybrida		x	x				x			x	
Antennaria	x						x		x		
Anthemis	x			x					x		Every other year
Aquilegia		x	x	x	(x)			x	x		
Arabis	x		x						x		
Arenaria		x		x	(x)	x			x	(x)	
Armeria	x		x	(x)	(x)				x		
Artemisia	x		x		x				x		Every year

[212]

Plant									Frequency of division
Aruncus		x						x	
Asclepias tuberosa	x							x	
Aster		x	x	x		(x)	x	x	Every other year
Astilbe		x	x					x	
Baptisia	x	x						x	
Belamcanda	x	x	(x)	(x)				x	
Bergenia	x	x		(x)				x	
Boltonia	x	x		(x)				x	Every other year
Brunnera		x						x	
Campanula	x	x	(x)					x	
Cassia marylandica									
Catananche		x	(x)	(x)	x			x	Alternate years
Centaurea	x	x	x	(x)				x	
Cerastium	x	x		x				x	
Ceratostigma	x	x	x	x				x	Every year
Chelone	x	x	x					x	
Chrysanthemum morifolium		(x)	(x)	(x)	(x)	(x)		x	Every year
C. coccineum		x	x	(x)		(x)		x	Every year
C. maximum		x	x	(x)		(x)		x	Alternate years
Cimicifuga		x	x					x	
Clematis		x	x					x	

[(x) indicates the characteristic may be highly variable]

	Dry Soil Conditions	Moist Soil Conditions	Intolerant of Wet Soil in Winter	Short-lived	Invasive	Hardiness Problems (Summer Heat)	Hardiness Problems (Winter Cold)	Serious Insect or Disease Problems	For Full Sun	Partial Shade	Require Frequent Division
Convallaria	x	x			x				x	x	
Coreopsis	x		(x)	(x)			(x)		x		
Delphinium		x	x	x			x	x	x		Every third year
Dianthus	x		x	(x)		(x)			x		
Dicentra	(x)	x			(x)				(x)	x	
Dictamnus		x							x		
Digitalis		x		x					x	x	
Doronicum		x							x	x	
Echinacea	x		x					(x)	x		
Echinops	x	x			x				x		
Epimedium		x								x	
Erigeron	x			x					x		
Eryngium	x		x				(x)		x		
Eupatorium		x			x				x	(x)	Alternate years
Euphorbia	x		x		(x)				x		
Filipendula	(x)	x							x	x	
Gaillardia	x		x	x			x		x		
Geranium		x			(x)				x	(x)	
Geum		x	x	(x)			(x)		x		
Gypsophila		x	x				(x)		x		
Helenium		x							x		

[214]

							Notes
Heliopsis	x					x	
Helleborus		x			x	x	
Hemerocallis	x		x		x	x	
Heuchera			x	(x)	x	x	
Hibiscus			x		x		
Hosta					x		
Iberis			x	(x)	x	x	
Iris siberica					x	x	
I. Japanese			x		x	(x)	
I. Bearded	(x)		x	x	x		Every third year
Kniphofia	x		x		x		
Liatris	x		x		x	x	
Ligularia			x		(x)	x	
Limonium	x				x		
Linum	x		x	(x)	x		
Lobelia			x	x	x	x	
Lupinus	x		x		x		
Lychnis	x		x	(x)	x		
Lysimachia	(x)		x	(x)	x	x	
Lythrum			x		x		
Macleaya	x		x	x	x	x	
Mertensia			x		x	x	
Monarda	x		x	x	x		(Every third year)
Nepeta	x		x	(x)	x	x	
Oenothera	x		x	(x)	(x)	x	Alternate years

[(x) indicates the characteristic may be highly variable]

	Dry Soil Conditions	Moist Soil Conditions	Intolerant of Wet Soil in Winter	Short-lived	Invasive	Hardiness Problems (Summer Heat)	Hardiness Problems (Winter Cold)	Serious Insect or Disease Problems	For Full Sun	Partial Shade	Require Frequent Division
Paeonia	x	x	x						x	(x)	
Papaver	x	x	x						x		
Phlox		x		(x)			(x)	x	x		Every third year
Physostegia	x	x			x				x		Alternate years
Platycodon	x	x	x						x		
Polemonium		x							x	x	
Polygonatum		x								x	
Primula		x	x	(x)		(x)		(x)		x	(Every third year)
Pulmonaria		x							x	x	
Rudbeckia	x	x	x		(x)				x		(Every third year)
Salvia	x	x	x	(x)			(x)		x		
Scabiosa		x	x						x		
Sedum	x	x	x				(x)		x		
Sidalcea		x	x						x		
Solidago	x	x							x		
Stachys	x	x	x						x	x	
Stokesia		x	x						x		
Thalictrum		x							x	x	

	1	2	3	4	5	6	7
Thermopsis	x					x	x
Tradescantia	x	x		(x)		x	x
Trollius	x	x				x	x
Verbascum		x		(x)		x	
Veronica		x				x	
Carex		x				x	
Elymus	x	x				x	
Erianthus	x	x				x	
Miscanthus	x	x				x	
Molinea	x	x	x			x	
Panicum		x	x			x	
Uniola		x		(x)		x	
Arrhenatherum	x	x				x	
Phalaris		x		x		x	
Spartina		x		(x)		x	x
Arundo		x		(x)	x	x	
Cortaderia		x			x	x	
Festuca	x	x				x	x

[217]

Acknowledgements

The author is grateful to colleagues and members of the Friends of the Arnold Arboretum for their assistance in the preparation of this guide. Dr. Gordon P. DeWolf, Jr., is responsible for the comprehensive tabular list of low maintenance perennials, and for portions of the chapter on culture. Mrs. Robert S. Blacklow spent many tedious hours carefully codifying the sources; Mrs. Frank Magullion put the primroses in their place, and offered constructive criticism of other portions of the manuscript, as did Drs. DeWolf and Richard E. Weaver, Jr. Mrs. Irving Fraim's lovely garden in Waltham was the setting for many of the photographs; other illustrations reflect the fine workmanship of artist Robert Opdyke.

To others, too numerous to mention, gratitude is due for their interest, encouragement, and knowledge freely shared. Without these contributions, large and small, Low Maintenance Perennials could not have become a reality.

ROBERT S. HEBB
Horticulturist, Cary Arboretum of
the New York Botanical Garden
(formerly Assistant Horticulturist,
Arnold Arboretum)

Erratum, page 107 — First two sentences under *Heuchera* should read:

These are excellent plants with few troubles, and capable of being left in place at least five years or longer before division will become necessary. They flower best in full sun, but also will perform well in light shade.

Index to Common Names

An attractive grouping of low maintenance perennials.